DATE DUE			

Our Secular Cathedrals:
Change and Continuity
In the University

OUR SECULAR CATHEDRALS: CHANGE AND CONTINUITY IN THE UNIVERSITY

The Franklin Lectures in the Sciences and Humanities

Third Series

ALAN RICHARDSON

DAVID RIESMAN

WALTER W. HELLER

DANIEL J. BOORSTIN

PHILIP HANDLER

LEON EDEL

Preface by Taylor Littleton

Published for
AUBURN UNIVERSITY
By
THE UNIVERSITY OF ALABAMA PRESS
University, Alabama

THE FRANKLIN LECTURES IN THE SCIENCES & HUMANITIES
Edited by Taylor Littleton

FIRST SERIES: *Approaching the Benign Environment,*
    by R. Buckminster Fuller, Eric A. Walker, James R. Killian, Jr.

SECOND SERIES: *The Shape of Likelihood: Relevance and the University.*
    by Loren Eiseley, Detlev W. Bronk, Jacob Bronowski, Howard Mumford Jones.

THIRD SERIES: *Our Secular Cathedrals: Change and Continuity in the University.*
    by Alan Richardson, David Riesman, Walter W. Heller, Daniel J. Boorstin Philip Handler, Leon Edel.

Contents

Contributors

Alan Richardson, Dean of York Cathedral, has taught at Oxford and Nottingham Universities and held a number of ecclesiastical posts. His influential works on theology and history include *History, Sacred and Profane* (the Bampton Lectures at Oxford in 1962); *Science, History and Faith; The Bible in the Age of Science;* and *Religion in Contemporary Debate.* A mark of his stature as a Biblical scholar is the inclusion of his essay "The Rise of Modern Biblical Scholarship" in the *Cambridge History of the Bible.*

David Riesman is America's foremost academic sociologist. Currently Henry Ford II Professor of Social Sciences at Harvard, his interpretations of American society and character are widely known *(The Lonely Crowd, Faces in the Crowd).* In recent years he has been especially interested in the sociology of higher education *(Constraint and Variety in American Education, The Academic Revolution).*

Walter Heller, one of the nation's best known economists, has published widely in the field of political economy and fiscal policy and has served as economic consultant in a variety of private and governmental agencies. In 1965–69 he served as Consultant to the Executive Office of the President and in 1961–64 was Chairman, President's Council of Economic Advisers. He is currently Regents' Professor of Economics at Minnesota.

Philip Handler, a distinguished biochemist and researcher, has held eminent positions throughout the scientific world. As president of the prestigious National Academy of Sciences, he is an influential force in the shaping and directing of our national priorities and research efforts in the sciences.

Daniel Boorstin, one of America's most perceptive social and intellectual historians, has earned his reputation through his distinguished career as teacher, principally at the University of Chicago, and through such distinctive publications as *The Lost World of Thomas Jefferson* (1948), *The Genius of American Politics* (1953), *America and the Image of Europe* (1960), and the highly complimented series entitled *The Americans (The Colonial Experience,* 1958; *The National Experience,* 1965; with the final volume in preparation). Dr. Boorstin is now Director of the Smithsonian Institution's National Museum of History and Technology.

Leon Edel holds distinguished professorial chairs at both New York University and the University of Hawaii. His multi-volume biography of Henry James is generally regarded as one of the finest works of literary scholarship produced in America. (The last volume, *Henry James: The Master,* was published in 1972.) Edel has also published works on James Joyce, Willa Cather, on the psychological novel, the art of literary biography, and the future prospects of the novel form. In 1963 he won the Pulitzer Prize for biography and in the same year the National Book Award for nonfiction.

Preface

IT IS A MINOR COINCIDENCE that these lectures are being prepared for publication at a time when the scholarly and scientific world is celebrating the anniversary dates of Nicolaus Copernicus and John Donne, whose careers bring to mind the uneasy relationship between science and humanistic thought in the modern world.

The Copernican theory, with its unsettling implications of an infinite universe and its possible displacement of earth and mankind as the center of God's divine attention, did not invade the popular imagination for a century. But the famous "undiscovered" star of 1572, as it blazed across the northern sky, seemed to many scientists to lend a certain credence to the new astronomy; and its study was a significant step toward the development of that world-view which would emerge more completely under the hands of Galileo, Bacon, and Newton. Donne himself was born in that year of scientific excitement, and his work strikingly illustrates that the new discoveries and their contradiction of tradition pervaded his thinking perhaps most strongly among early seventeenth century poets. His poetry, as every undergraduate knows, illustrates again and again a reconstruction of disparate elements and experiences into a new order of personal and humane expression, as though bearing witness to an individual intellect making its unique progress within a confused and uncertain cosmos.

Copernicus and Donne, then, born a century apart, form a powerful historical image of the two-dimensional experience that has increasingly defined our common life and that, to some extent, finds a commemorative statement in the essays contained in this volume. On the one hand, Philip Handler, Walter Heller, and Daniel Boorstin—each in his own way—discuss the expansive world of science, technology, economics, and politics enclosing our individual destinies. And, on the other, Leon Edel and Boorstin speak eloquently of how this macrocosmic order impinges on the smaller community of individual and familiar relationships, a community threatened by the attenuation of experience and by the kaleidoscopic confusion presented to the imagination by the media and its technology. Indeed, to Edel, the sun in the Copernican universe—the great eye of heaven—would today find its metaphysical reduction in the screen of the television set.

The volume opens with two essays, one by a widely known Biblical scholar and the other by a distinguished sociologist, that are illustrative of the book's title. Alan Richardson's is a classic statement of the humanistic emphases of the university as a force in history and of the twin ideals of *humanitas* and *universitas*, while David Riesman, from whose essay the term "secular cathedrals" is taken, develops an analysis of the various cultural conflicts that have altered the idea of continuity discussed by Richardson. Taken together, the two present a concept of change and continuity that is, to be sure, an ongoing process within the secular cathedral.

Riesman's wise and perceptive comments, developed within an auditorium dialogue with hundreds of students and faculty, seem to recapture the whole troubled landscape of the 6o's. Thus, his statements form a proper entree to the essays that follow, essays whose very titles suggest issues of considerable interest in the contemporary university setting. They illustrate, in fact, not only the rich multiplicity of thought inherent in the "changing" university described by Riesman but also reveal there the "continuity" of humane concerns discussed by Richardson.

Hopefully, then, readers of this book will perceive among these essays thematic relationships of the kind suggested here. It may well be that reverential attitudes toward the secular cathedral are waning somewhat in the 1970's; the "new men" of the current university scene are the academic managers whose task is to assess productivity and develop accountability systems.

Even so, many of the great concerns and issues of our time still find their most characteristic expression and analysis within the university, as the statements of these six Lecturers illustrate. The intertwining of our existence with the powers of science has, as Handler makes clear, never been greater. And the ecology of our imagination, together with the character of our national life, has never been more imperiled. Our own perception of the continuing vitality of the university and of the great correspondence between science and humanity will be deepened by these essays. And perhaps as suggested above, the effect will attain a certain relevance as we remember Copernicus and Donne in this, their anniversary season.

Auburn University   Taylor Littleton
March, 1973

xi

Alan Richardson

History, Humanity, and University

Alan Richardson

History, Humanity, and University

THERE IS A SENSE in which the historical consciousness of a people, a nation, or a social group is the
most important thing about it. The historical experience of any nation or group has determined what it
is today and what will be its reactions to the crises
and opportunities of every new age. Peoples differ
from other peoples because of their different histories.
Foreignness means not sharing the historical experience of a particular people. It is therefore not surprising that reverence for the past as the matrix in which
present existence was shaped should be characteristic
of civilization from the earliest times. Even before the
dawn of their literary history the ancient Greeks, for
example, had created for themselves a richly imagina-
tive mythological and legendary prehistory by means
of which they could explain the mystery of their own
existence to themselves. When the literary stage of
a people's evolution has been reached, historians take
over from the poets the function of interpreting the

3

nation's existence to itself, creating the self-understanding which confers upon a people its sense of belonging to this particular human association and not to any other. I think that something of this kind was in the mind of the American historian Carl Becker when in his famous essay of 1910 he wrote: "We historians are of that ancient and honorable company of wise men of the tribe ... to whom in successive ages has been entrusted the keeping of the useful myths."[1]

In this sense every developed nation has its historians; that is, literary men who interpret the meaning of ther people's existence in the very act of writing its history. It is in this sense that history-writing is inevitably a matter of interpretation, the imputation of some kind of meaning, the recognition of some kind of character or even destiny, in the people whose history is being told. It matters little whether the historian is conscious of his function as interpreter or 'wise man of the tribe'. Before the rise of the conception of 'scientific history' in the nineteenth century, it was taken for granted that history was written "to point a moral and adorn a tale." But the nineteenth century itself demonstrated that the ideal of purely scientific history ('wie es eigentlich gewesen') was a chimaera: the greatest of the 'scientific' historians, Leopold von Ranke, himself turned out to be the interpreter or myth-maker of the Prussian State.[2]

The Hebrew Experience

Long before the birth of Herodotus (c. B.C. 485–426), the putative 'father of history', the Hebrew consciousness was saturated with the sense of the strength that

4

is derived from history. In every crisis of Israel's history the prophetic mind turned to the past for inspiration and guidance. "Hearken unto me, ye that follow after righteousness; look unto the rock whence ye were hewn and to the hole of the pit whence ye were digged. Look unto Abraham your father and to Sarah who bore you...." (Isa. 51. 1f.). "We have heard with our ears, O God, our fathers have told us, the work which thou didst perform in their days" (Ps. 44.1). Biblical religion in fact differs from all the other varieties of the world's religions in being historical in character; it bases its claim to knowledge of the truth upon things which have happened in history, upon events which have actually passed before the eyes of men and which have been attested by witnesses. In particular the recognition of God as the Lord of history took its origin in a sequence of stirring events by which Israel's national existence was determined: the exodus from Egypt, the deliverance at the Red Sea, the covenant-making at Sinai, and the entry into the Promised Land. The prophets of Israel in the eighth to the sixth centuries B.C. appeal again and again to the historical deliverance at the Red Sea, to the trusting obedience to Jehovah of the People in the desert, and to the covenant and promise which they had made with Jehovah to the exclusion of every heathen baal. Be true, they say to their own generation, be faithful to your history, and the God of your fathers will be your God and you will be his people. Without the happening at the Red Sea there would have been no Israel, no prophetic voice among the nations, no knowledge in the world of a God of righteousness, no people to make ready the coming of a Messiah, no New Covenant ratified in the blood of the Paschal Lamb of the New Israel, when he came in the fullness of time.

Israel is the supreme example of a people which drew strength from her own history; she has provided a paradigm of historical existence as such, and other nations have learnt from her how to interpret their own historical existence. Thus, St. Augustine learned from Jeremiah how to understand the sack of Rome by Alaric the Goth in A.D. 410: Rome had not fallen because she had been deserted by the goddess Fortuna, offended at the neglect of her shrines in favor of an oriental deity called Jehovah; Rome, "the great western Babylon," had fallen because the God of all the earth was a God of righteousness. Or again, it is recorded that when Karl Barth was conducted round the ruins of Berlin after 1945, he quoted Isaiah 26.9: "When the judgments of God are in the earth, the inhabitants of the world learn righteousness." It is not, however, only for times of disaster that Israel's history provides later ages with paradigms; there are models of hope and promise as well as of judgment and catastrophe. The promise held out to Israel on pilgrimage towards the promised land has again and again in the Christian centuries been the inspiration of the quest for a better order of things. If one might venture an illustration from American history, the noble ideals of the Declaration of Independence or those moving words inscribed on Bertholdi's statue of "Liberty enlightening the world" in New York harbor are still relevant and still compelling in such an age as ours, when the path towards liberty and equality seems harder and steeper than it was thought to be in 1776 or 1886. The cynics and the defeatists may have lost heart; the irresolute may have turned aside to worship the golden calf; but still in our days prophetic voices bid the pilgrim people, who would follow after righteousness, to look to the rock whence they were hewn, to follow in spite of every failure and discouragement in the direction in which their own history points.

Classical Humanism

The Hebraic contribution to the shaping of our European or Western civilization consisted essentially in its recognition of the historical character of human existence. The other great contributory stream was the classical tradition of Greece and Rome. The Hebrew and the classical traditions flowed together and became a mighty river in the Christian civilization of the high Middle Ages. This surprising confluence of biblical faith and classical philosophy has been strikingly expressed by the late Professor A. O. Lovejoy: "The God of Aristotle had almost nothing in common with the God of the Sermon on the Mount—though by one of the strangest and most momentous paradoxes of Western history, the philosophical theology of Christendom identified them, and defined the chief end of man as the imitation of both."[3] Many students of the history of thought are convinced that, apart from this confluence of the Greek and the Hebraic, the emergence of modern empirical science could not have taken place. However that may be, the fact remains that it was out of late mediaeval thought in Western Europe that modern scientific method was evolved; it is to the high civilization of the late Middle Ages that we owe the development of technology and of

7

modern scientific medicine and agriculture, blessings which the whole world is willing to receive from the West, even though it may reject so many of the values and assumptions of contemporary Western civilization.

One of the movements of thought which greatly assisted the transition from the mediaeval to the modern (or scientific) way of looking at things is known as 'humanism'. In its strict and proper sense the word means education based upon the Greek and Latin classics.[4] The Latin word *humanitas* ('the human race', 'mankind') denotes the distinctively human or moral attitude of one human being towards another: benevolence, philanthropy, courtesy, and politeness. We might contrast 'inhuman', meaning cruel, callous, criminal. In the ancient world humanity was a virtue to be exercised towards one's fellow-citizens; it did not extend to inferiors, such as slaves, or to aliens. In Christian civilization it was extended to all men irrespective of race or rank or condition; indeed, humanity was especially to be shown towards the sick, the aged, the poor and the defenseless—even to animals. The word 'humanitarian' came to denote the attitude of the Good Samaritan.

Those fine scholars who rediscovered ancient culture, the renaissance humanists, created the atmosphere in which the emergent modern scientific movement could breathe. They learnt from the great minds of antiquity how to exercise the critical faculties which had for so long been dormant, because mediaeval philosophers had come to regard the writings of Aristotle as being second only to the Holy Scriptures in their inspiration and authority. Aristotle's scientific opinions were dogmatically upheld by the Inquisition, and to question them was almost equal in gravity to the sin of doubting the revealed truths of the Bible, as Galileo discovered. Galileo was beginning to understand what every schoolboy knows today, that stones do not fall to the ground, as Aristotle taught, because they want to go home, but because the physical universe is governed by natural laws which can be calculated with mathematical precision. The development of natural science could never have taken place if the mythological Aristotelian physics had not been deposed from the position of honor accorded to all the works of 'the Philosopher' in the later Middle Ages. The important matter for us to notice is that it was the revival of classical studies by the humanists of the fourteenth and fifteenth centuries which made possible the rise of the modern scientific movement. The humanist scholars sharpened their wits and improved their critical methods by their study of classical literature and philosophy; if it is going too far to say that they used Aristotle to cast out Aristotle, at least we might say that they absorbed from their renewed classical studies much of the questioning, critical spirit of antiquity. They acquired a temper of mind to which all dogmatism was abhorrent and all questions were open to discussion. This enquiring attitude of the humanists not only rendered inevitable the Reformation; it also made possible the development of the scientific world-view.

The clever Greeks did not invent natural science, though all the sciences have Greek names. In the opinion of many historians of thought, they could not have done so, because their minds were dominated by deep subconscious irrational fears of fate and chance and luck and necessity; it was essential that the demons of the underworld of the Greek mind should be exorcized by the serene Christian trust in a God of order, purpose, and love, before the genius of the Greeks could make its unique and lasting contribution to the development of civilization. The formulation of modern scientific method could have been achieved only in a civilization which had in spite of all improbability fused together the God of Aristotle with the God of the Sermon on the Mount, a union which Professor Lovejoy found so paradoxical. At any rate no other of the world's great civilizations did in fact formulate and employ the methods of inductive science which have transformed the face of the whole earth and which today promise—or threaten—to change the face of the heavens as well.

From these considerations certain conclusions follow. First, it becomes obvious that the humane tradition, or the study of the humanities, was essential to the birth and progress of science and the scientific attitude. A succession of remarkable scholars, from the Italian Petrarch (1304–74), 'the first modern man', to Erasmus (1467–1536), 'the European man', recovered the enquiring spirit, the urbane and tolerant skepticism and the aversion to dogmatism of the rarest spirits of the ancient world. They virtually founded a whole new system of education based upon the classical tradition, the Greek *paideia*. They exposed the pious forgeries which provided ancient authority for mediaeval innovations; they taught men to scoff at claims to authority based on ignorance and superstition; they showed that questions which had long been considered closed because 'the Philosopher' had spoken might be opened and discussed again; in short they created the atmosphere in which the new experimental science could breathe. In a word, the humanists of the Renaissance made possible the achievements of Copernicus, Kepler, Galileo and the rest. It follows from these considerations that the doctrine of the 'two cultures' recently propagated by Lord Snow is mistaken. There is only one culture and the humanities are the necessary foundation and condition of free scientific enquiry and of progress in the sciences.[5]

One further conclusion follows from the line of thought which we have been pursuing. The European tradition of humanity is itself a signal illustration of the way in which strength is derived from history. The Renaissance humanists were indeed looking to the rock whence they were hewn and to the hole of the pit whence they were digged; and in their case it was to the spirit of free enquiry which they were looking, the spirit which had found expression in the philosophers and dramatists, the poets and historians, of Greece and subsequently of Rome. The recovery of ancient truth is often the condition of the discovery of new lines of advance. The Greeks did not invent natural science, but the recovery of the Greek ideal of free enquiry was the condition of the invention of scientific method in the modern world. And this essential condition was met by the labors of the Christian humanists of the Renaissance.

Humanity and Freedom

There are, of course, other spheres than that of the natural sciences in which the tradition of humanity has played a role of decisive importance. There is, for example, the whole field of literature: which European literature has not received a large part of its inspiration and its form from classical antiquity, whatever may have been the contribution of some original Germanic or other 'barbarian' stock? But we must not pursue this vast subject now, because the question of humanity and society, or of the humane tradition in politics, is more immediately relevant to our purpose. Today it is especially necessary to realize that the vitality of the humane tradition is a necessary condition of the continuance of free scientific enquiry and of academic freedom in general. Whenever the humane tradition is rejected, as in Nazi Germany or in Soviet-occupied Europe today, such scientists and literary men as are not in prison or the labor-camps become puppets of the State. The custodians of the humane tradition, notably the universities and the churches, must first be destroyed so that there will be no challenge to the philosophy which the rulers find convenient. There are indeed institutions in totalitarian societies which are still called universities, but they are no longer places where the spirit of free enquiry can exist; they are state-controlled institutions designed for the production of the docile operatives who are needed to run the state enterprises of industry, defense, health-services, research, administration, etc. 'The Party' is the natural enemy of humanity. The Institute of Scientific Atheism must be set up as a kind of anti-church, because even after a half-century of atheistic propaganda the security of the ruling group is threatened if anything of the humane tradition survives. It is no accident that when dictators desire to bring the universities into line they begin by abolishing the departments of classics and theology and purging the departments of history and literature.[6] History must be rewritten to show that its true fulfilment has been attained in the totalitarian state, and literature must be subjected to censorship in order to protect the citizens from erroneous teaching. Only then will it be possible to ensure that all students, including the scientists and technologists, are carefully instructed in philosophy; that is, the rationalization which will justify the seizure and retention of power by the ruling group.

Because the tradition of humanity still lingers amongst us, we in the West are filled with revulsion: indoctrination and compulsion deprive the individual of his essential humanity by preventing him from thinking for himself and from speaking his own thoughts. We do not want indoctrination here, and in any case we have no agreed philosophy to inculcate; ours is an open society, a pluralist commonwealth, not a monolithic pyramid of power. Now it is true that we have no agreed dogmatic philosophy such as Aristotelian scholasticism or Marxist materialism, but this does not mean that we in the West have no convictions at all. It would be more accurate to speak of our deep moral conviction rather than of any articulated philosophy. This conviction lies at the center of our whole university experience and is the living heart of the humane tradition. It may be stated in this way. Truth and value can be apprehended—made a person's own—only when they have been freely discovered, freely chosen and freely loved. Freedom of choice is the *conditio sine qua non* of being human;

responsible freedom is what differentiates the human from every other species. Dogmas can be indoctrinated, but truth and value cannot. Prepackaged answers to all the questions about man and society can be handed out by authority to the young, but truth cannot be assimilated except through being personally chosen. This is the conviction that compelled the Renaissance humanists to challenge the dogmatic authoritarianism of their day; and they had acquired this conviction, as we have noted, through their renewed study of the classical writers.

The Renaissance humanists of the fourteenth to the sixteenth centuries, of whom we have spoken, played an essential role in the development of the humane tradition of academic freedom without which the university as we understand it in the West could not have come into being and could not continue to exist. But, of course, the reawakening of the spirit of free enquiry had begun in the West long before the fourteenth century. Historians nowadays remind us that there were several renaissances, not just one Renaissance. The Middle Ages do not in fact constitute a thousand-year period of dogmatic lethargy, as used to be supposed: they were the inevitably long period of the rebuilding of civilization after the dark age of the barbarian invasions. One of the most characteristic and abiding achievements of this Middle Age was the evolution of the university with its tradition of academic freedom. That tradition did not develop easily. It arose largely in connection with the transition from the older type of 'monastic' theology to the new type of 'scholastic' theology in the twelfth century renaissance, forever associated with the name of Peter Abelard (1079–

1142).[7] The older theology had considered it impious to discuss the reasonableness of the deliverances of the Scriptural revelation: reason could not be set up as a judge of revealed truth. This was the position of St. Bernard of Clairvaux, the last great representative of the so-called 'monastic' type of theology, who secured the papal condemnation of Abelard and his new-style theology but who nevertheless failed to prevent Abelard's 'new' theology from becoming the accepted 'style' of all future theology: namely, a seeking to understand by means of reason itself what the deliverances of the Scriptures or the pronouncements of the Fathers really meant for us as rational beings. From our twentieth century standpoint, most of us would not feel at home with either Bernard or Abelard; but that is irrelevant. The fact remains that Abelard carried the day: truth was what the freely operating human reason could perceive to be true, and in that conviction the university tradition of free academic enquiry developed and passed into the very fabric of the European experience. By the end of the twelfth century three universities of distinction had emerged, Paris, Bologna, and Oxford: they were the prototypes of the universities, the bearers of academic freedom, which today are established throughout all five continents. As Sir Charles Grant Robertson, a distinguished former Vice-Chancellor of an English university, has pointed out, the whole apparatus of faculties, degrees, matriculations, gowns, hoods, vice-chancellors, professors, deans, and so on, today bears witness to the mediaeval achievement of building a Latin-Christian culture on a Greek foundation: "Without this creation by the mediaeval mind, the bridge from Greek, Roman, Jew-

15

ish, and Arabic culture, literature, and science could never have been built. Newton, Darwin, Pasteur, and Einstein were made possible by Abelard and Thomas Aquinas, as were also Erasmus, Luther, and Calvin, Descartes, Pascal, Locke, and Kant."[8]

The Universality of the Humane Tradition

The very word *universitas* implies the unity of all scholarly endeavor, the cooperation of all workers in the search for knowledge, and the ultimate unity of every field of human enquiry in a common universe of knowledge. The university is concerned with man in his total environment, cosmic, physical, geological, biological, historical, and social; it is concerned not only with his environment but with his inner, existential being, psychological, personal, and spiritual. The twin ideals of *humanitas* and *universitas* are the connecting links, forged in the Middle Ages, between the achievements of ancient civilization and those of the modern Western world. Sometimes it is said that this insistence upon the Western or European character of the humane tradition is unattractive to peoples of non-European traditions, for example, in Asia and Africa; to them the humane tradition seems to be only a disguise for Western cultural imperialism. The argument can be made to sound very plausible. Why should Africans study the alien literature of Greeks, Romans, and Hebrews? What has Accra to do with Athens or Ibadan with Jerusalem? The answer, of course, is the same for Africans as for Englishmen or Americans: there is only one humanity. The humane tradition belongs to the whole human race, and to cut ourselves off from it is to diminish our human stature. The fact is that universities with a genuinely humane tradition are now established across the world from the West Indies to Malaysia, and their very existence bears powerful witness to the appeal of the university idea to men of many races and cultures. If this dispersion means anything at all, it points to the truth that there is only one humanity: there are many cultures, and each has its own excellence, but there is only one humanity. Nor should we forget that the mediaeval synthesis garnered not only the fruits of Greek and Latin culture but also the moral dynamic of the Hebrews, the wisdom of the Arabian philosophers (who had rediscovered Aristotle), and through them the great advances of the Indian mathematicians. Newton could hardly have produced his *Principia Mathematica* if the only systems of numerical notation which he had known had been those of the Greeks and Romans. The humane tradition has always been ready to assimilate new truth from whatever quarter it has come.

Yet today it must be admitted that all is not well with the humane tradition. It is not merely that it is despised and rejected throughout the Marxist third of the world. Far more serious is the lack of confidence shown by the Western (or Westernized) world during the last decade or so. Something happened to the West during the sixties. That 'something' seems akin to what happened to the Graeco-Roman world during the early Christian centuries. Professor Gilbert Murray once described it as a "failure of nerve."[9] The second and third centuries A.D. were an age of 'death of God theologies': the ancient verities seemed to have lost their compelling power and the old Roman virtues seemed no longer attractive. Though ostensibly the Roman Empire collapsed through the invasions of the barbarians from without, those alien incursions were successful only because of the decay of the old Roman virtues from within. Something similar to this process may be happening to Western-type civilization today. The young, especially the student generation, seem alienated from the resources which Western nations generally have found in history and in tradition. The old sources of inspiration seem to have turned sour. All at once there is revolt against the structures of capitalist (or semi-socialist) society, now declared to be legalized violence in the interest of the oppressors. The 'obscene structures of society' must be destroyed, if necessary by violence. The university, especially in its scientific and technological departments, is the servant of repressive capitalism, because it trains the élite upon which the whole system depends. It is necessary to involve the mass of the people in the revolutionary struggle; and if one is in the university, that is where one must begin.

Thus it has come about, for reasons not easy to explain, that thousands of students in several of the most famous universities of the world have become estranged from the humane tradition. It may be that the institutions to which they belong have so failed to embody that tradition in their constitution and in their practice that they have no clear idea of what it is. They turn away, perhaps as a definite gesture of rejection, from the tradition of the West to oriental mystical techniques, or to the latter-day romanticism of Herbert Marcuse with his vision of a repressionless society, or, more grossly, to violence or drugs. They dismiss the humane tradition as a liberal illusion, preferring 'contestation' (a word not found in English dictionaries, meaning 'contestation idéologique'), that is, the refutation of capitalist and bourgeois ideology. Like all revolutionaries they want to forget the past and to destroy the records of it: the past is so repellent that the study of history itself should be proscribed.[10] But, as Lord Acton noted, it is precisely in periods of revolutionary thought and action that the significance of the past is rediscovered and history is reborn.[11] Perhaps it is in this reflection that those of us who cherish the humane tradition and look for its reactivization in the university world of tomorrow may actually find grounds for hope. Tides ebb as rapidly as they flow and student moods change swiftly. Values which seem to have been lost have a habit of reappearing, and if we are right in holding that the tradition of humanity has arisen out of the very nature and constitution of human existence as such, it is not necessary for us to abandon hope in the future of the humane tradition and therefore in the future of the human race itself.

Thus, in our present confused situation, if we ask where is wisdom to be found and where is the place of understanding, I believe that the answer is contained in the prophetic word of Scripture: "Hearken to me, ye that follow after righteousness, ye that seek the Lord: look unto the rock whence ye were hewn, and to the hole of the pit whence ye were digged." Look carefully at the humane tradition of respect for personality, of readiness to listen to and to discuss the views of those with whom we disagree or from

whom we have become estranged. By all means look
at the many failures to embody the idea in the institution, to exhibit humanity in the university, but consider
how despite its failures there has again and again been
recovery and renewal, as for instance after 1945 in
Germany, where academic freedom had apparently
perished in the country of its highest development.
Communications must be kept open, new bridges must
be built, between members of the university and civic
communities across all barriers of ideology, race, religion, status, or age. Above all, each of us must hold
fast to his own convictions, especially those deep moral
convictions which truly establish our personal identity
within the community. For without moral conviction
men are something less than human, having lost all
title to be the bearers of the tradition of humanity.

[1]"Detachment and the Writing of History" in the *Atlantic
Monthly*, Oct. 1910.

[2]This statement is expanded in my *History Sacred and
Profane*, 1964, 172–183.

[3]A. O. Lovejoy, *The Great Chain of Being*, 1942, 5.

[4]Hence we speak of 'the humanities' or 'humane studies'
(*studia humaniora*), *litterae humaniores* (classical studies),
or (in the Scottish Universities) Professors of Humanity,
i.e. Latin.

[5]Another illustration of this truth may be derived from
the reflection that the Darwinian hypothesis of organic
evolution could not (and certainly did not) receive formulation until the nineteenth-century revolution in historical
method had familiarized the European mind with the conception of real evolutionary development in the passage
of the centuries.

[6]See Hans-Gerhard Koch, *The Abolition of God*, 1963, a study of the European atheist tradition with special reference to Marxist-Leninist developments.

[7]See Leif Grane, *Peter Abelard: Philosophy and Christianity in the Middle Ages*, Engl. trans., 1970.

[8]*Chambers' Encyclopaedia*, ed. 1950, XIV, 193a.

[9]Cf. the superb chapter bearing this title in his *Five Stages of Greek Religion*, 1925.

[10]*Lectures on Modern History*, 1907, 14.

[11]See my *History Sacred and Profane*, 1964, 166.

David Riesman

*Cultural Conflict in the University**

*I would like to acknowledge the assistance of the Ford Foundation and the Carnegie Corporation in support of my work on problems of higher education reflected in this address—D. R.

David Riesman

Cultural Conflict In The University

INTRODUCTORY NOTE

*I had explained to my host, Dean Taylor Littleton, that
I prefer never simply to give a lecture and let it go at
that; I wanted to be sure to have ample time for discussion following my address. I believe that what I
have in mind can only become clear as the result of
an ensuing discussion; this is especially the case at a
new place, as Auburn was for me, this being my first
visit to Alabama. The lecture hour started a bit late;
consequently, in order to have discussion within the
hour, I sharply truncated my remarks. In what follows, I have filled in some of what got left out. In the
discussion, as seems unavoidable, the questions were
often inaudible; sometimes I have reconstructed them
from scratch, and other times trust the bearing of the
question will be clear from my responses; and these,
too, have been somewhat edited to repair gaps and
also to clarify obscurities. What cannot here be repro-
duced is the several further days of discussion following the lecture, during which I had two partic-*

ularly intense meetings with Auburn's quotient of more assertively radical and liberal students who had strong objections to some of the things I had said. In speaking on controversial topics to a diverse and unknown audience, it is difficult to avoid lending whatever weight one has to what may locally be majority sentiment, if one is concerned with one's own beliefs and not merely with their instant impact locally. Yet in a way, as I said to them, I envied Auburn's more outspoken liberal and radical faculty and students because their very isolation in a state governed by George Wallace left them in no doubt as to who their enemies were. Correspondingly, however, this very situation of exposure, even danger, gave some of them the feeling that, if one was not with them on all fronts, one was after all in the position of supporting their enemies.

Some Auburn witnesses to these discussions told me later that they thought some of the students had been "unsouthern" in the fierceness of their attacks on me and their departure from the norms of southern civility and politeness. I knew what they had in mind. Still, in contrast to what one can find on the elite northern campus, I found the general level of discourse extremely civil and reflective; it stays with me now, seven months after the original events.

One of the things that brings me to Auburn is my continuing interest in the enormous diversity of American higher education and my relative lack of experience with education in the Deep South. I had the experience a few weeks ago of being visited by a Dutch educator who had been sent for a year to the United States by the Dutch Ministry of Higher Education to study the American system or, as I called it, the non-system, in order to see what might be done in the Netherlands to increase the proportion of post-secondary students to something like the American level. He was interested in American community colleges—in the whole extensive range of American academia. It perplexed him, as it perplexes many non-American visitors, to discover how unhappy many American colleges and university students are when, by the standards of the Continent, there is so much more openness, so much more room. He explained to me that the thirty universities in Holland are built, whether nominally private or public, pretty much on the same ground-plan. Each has virtually the same set of departments; none has overshadowing prestige. In some ways he felt this an improvement on the more centralized situation in France where Paris has hegemony, or Japan where Tokyo and Kyoto have hegemony.

But all these Continental systems are in one vital respect different from the American arrangement where each institution competes, always locally and sometimes also nationally, for its very survival and growth. None of them, even the most eminent, is given, so to speak, on the landscape. Auburn University is, of course, a land-grant institution, but this does not mean that it controls a particular patch of academic turf which unequivocally assures it of a particular flow of students, faculty, staff, or support.

When Alexis de Tocqueville came to the United States in 1831 he had as a French Catholic nobleman a very different attitude toward Catholicism in a non-

Catholic country than did most Frenchmen or Spaniards or Italians who visited the United States. Rather than thinking it was terrible that there was no established Catholic Church whose parishes were part of a patrimony of everyone, Tocqueville thought it marvelous that the parish priests had to be "hustlers"; indeed, they had to be entrepreneurs. Their parish was not given as a territorial right. He felt that American Catholicism flourished precisely because it was not established.

The same is true of American higher education. The college president has to be a hustler, and it does not matter whether it is Birmingham-Southern, Spring Hill, Auburn, Tuscaloosa, or even Troy State—he has to see that the bills are paid, that the customers come, and that the faculty aren't too miserable with these customers. And as a rule between the customers or patrons from whom the resources flow and the intellectuals or academicians who are paid for their care and feeding, there is always a certain tension.

To be sure, at the different levels and locales of academia, these tensions are unevenly reflected. To give an example, I had thought before my visit that Troy State might flourish because Auburn and Tuscaloosa attracted students who wrote for the *Crimson and White* or the *Plainsman* and said things not universally popular in the state. I had had the impression based on experience in other states, as well as on limited reading, that when the state university and the land-grant university are thought of as dissonant, the newer and especially the regional state colleges and universities, such as Troy State or the University of Southern Alabama in Mobile, might take the occasion to flourish at the expense of the older and more distinguished places. This may in some measure be happening, but it was a mistake on my part to suppose that community colleges (as Christopher Jencks and I prophesied in chapter two of *The Academic Revolution*) would prosper as the war between the generations increased in intensity. For even in the community colleges, the conflicts that rage in our nation and culture may be reflected. The student who goes home at night from a commuter college in Buffalo or Detroit may carry with him or her a vision of Catholicism very different from that of the parish priest and that of the, let us say, Polish parental family. Indeed an inner city community college is likely to reflect the diverse ethnic mix of its locale and hence, at least in many northern cities, to reflect the precarious balance among white and non-white students. But such conflicts, seemingly racial, may reflect the social-class backgrounds of the students, and as well the social-class backgrounds of the faculty.

And indeed, on the faculty side, because something is called a college, the faculty are likely to value not only their local ties, their provincial roots, but also ties to their discipline which is worldwide, to their guild, and to the non-local orbits of their own potential visibility.

People like myself who study higher education have talked about the difference between faculty members who are "locals" and are oriented to the institution and loyal to it, and faculty members who are "cosmopolitans," loyal to their guild, for whom the institution is only a base, a resting place until the next and better job turns up. But in fact that is too gross a distinction, for one finds in many places "home-guard cosmopolitans"—people with both local attachments and national ties. They have local attachments because they are attracted to their department or to their students or both, to where they live, to where their wives live; and they also have national ties to the networks of their guild even beyond the boundaries of the nation. Indeed, I have thought of myself as a home-guard cosmopolitan both when I taught at Chicago and now at Harvard; for I have been deeply committed to the institutions, and to undergraduate education. Limited energies and occasional conflicts of concern, if not of interest, mean that the tension between local and cosmopolitan values is something many of us experience.

On the whole the cosmopolitan side of things has grown at the expense of the locals since the end of the Second World War. The years following the end of the Second World War have been boom years for academia. There has been an incredible increase in undergraduate customers since that time; this in turn has permitted a pyramiding of graduate and professional programs, expecially as the states and regions in America competed with each other for academic distinction. An indication of that growth is the fact that in many cities the largest employer is the local university. Memphis State is bigger than National Harvester, in Memphis. Auburn, of course, *is* the University. And some of our larger universities bring more people together in one place than anything in the country except an Army camp or General Motors.

The contribution to the growth of universities in the post-Second-World-War era of science and space is no news to anyone in Alabama, whether in Huntsville or here, and the deliquescence of that advance is also no news. In the post-sputnik era, science and scholarship were seen as both socially useful and humanly attractive. And in a democracy the assumption was made that anybody who could do the work, whether as learner or teacher or researcher, could get a job. And to be a trustee or benefactor of an educational institution appeared until very recently more attractive than similar relation to other public facilities, such as mental hospitals or our jails. The state universities and their land-grant rivals have been our secular cathedrals.

Ethnic and religious communities, in order to compete with these secular cathedrals, have had to build their own, so that we have the twenty-seven varieties of Jesuit college of which Spring Hill in your state is an example, thus partially incorporating within themselves the secular religion of higher education. And I need not tell Southerners about the many Baptist institutions stretching from Furman to Baylor and west and south. Only such small anti-educational closed groups as the Amish and the Hutterites stayed out of the procession. In effect, they said to their adolescents: if you stay with us, we will give you a farm and a good barn and we will stock it; but if you leave the fold, you will have to enter the (probably urban) labor force at the very bottom.

Regions of the country, as well as ethnic and religious groups, have competed with each other in the increasingly national arena of higher education. Thus, the Southern and Mountain States have been expending staggering amounts, on a per capita basis, to expand

31

their educational systems in part to limit the brain drain which has drawn so many talented youngsters, for instance, out of the South (and brought in many Yankee migrants), and in part as a matter of pride in state and inter-regional competition. It is a pride in which football prowess has sometimes been the loss-leader for academic prowess.

In Willie Morris's autobiography, *North Toward Home*, he describes how astonished he was when he went from Yazoo City to the University of Texas to discover that one could get paid for reading books and for studying. To enter the digs of a graduate student whose walls were lined with books that were not even required reading was thrilling. He attended college in the post-World War II era when the Gentleman's C began to lose favor, and study became in effect a major sport on many campuses.

One consequence has been that academic men became more influential than they had previously been in America, and often more influential than they realized. They began to influence large managerial business, while still being opposed and regarded as soft-headed by small business—small in terms of complexity but not always in terms of profitability. (Of course, there are exceptions both ways: not all big businessmen are liberal nor all small businessmen provincial.) Similarly, academic men became more influential in the Federal government and, in varying degrees, in state and local government. Many natural and some social scientists became more worldly. Over the years, in occasionally visiting state universities, I have asked whether there is resentment of the fact that the president and perhaps a good many faculty members, especially in the medical school, may be paid a larger salary than the governor or any state official. Surprisingly, there has been little resentment of this.

Furthermore, state universities could use national sources of support to build programs not responsive to what influential people in the state might consider advantageous. One could imagine, for instance, that former Senator Lister Hill might have been a more important friend of Auburn than, let us say, the head of the state Department of Education or a member of a particular committee in the state legislature. By mobilizing external support, colleges and universities were able to diversify their own offerings, while paradoxically becoming more like their competitors. Thus the land-grant universities could serve the state and acquire a certain amount of political power through the network of county agents, while also building their liberal arts programs to compete with the state university—which in turn might be building a school of engineering to compete with that on the land-grant campus.

All booms must come to an end sometime, and the growth in what has been called the knowledge industry has had to slow down. What we have seen happening since the late 1960's can be called an academic recession or deflation or indeed the Depression of '69, depending on where one stands in the academic landscape and on how durable one expects the deceleration to be. The impact of course has been uneven. A great many private colleges and universities, including some very notable ones, are close to bankruptcy. And many of the more eminent state universities wonder how they can maintain their libraries and laboratories in a period of not only relatively but sometimes absolutely shrinking resources. Furthermore, expectations have kept on rising even while resources have started to fall off. Both faculties and students want smaller classes, more services and fringe benefits, even while the administration wonders how it can meet the next payroll and how long the under-maintenance of plant can go on without a scandal, or even a disaster. Institutions are expected to respond to what are newly defined as problems even while they cannot relinquish tenured faculty in fields that no longer have allure.

Part of the decline in funding can of course be traced to the "adult backlash"—the reaction of parents, legislators, taxpayers against campus protests and social unrest generally. But even less troubled campuses have been affected by these reactions. What we are seeing is a massive loss of faith in progress itself, a loss of faith that higher education is necessarily a good thing, either for particular individuals or for society as a whole. We have no good measures of the "productivity" of higher education, and many people have come to believe that a dollar spent on Head Start may go further than a dollar spent on a new university program.

If these attitudes were found only outside the universities, they would be serious enough. But my particular interest here is in discussing the disintegration of the old belief in progress, the belief that things are getting better, among many thousands of faculty members and students. I have encountered such attitudes even in such temples of science and engineering as the California Institute of Technology. Even before the present difficulties outstanding scientists and engineers have had in getting jobs.

We Americans are now intensely and unavoidably aware of all the disasters that may befall the planet. There was a time when, if there was a riot in Harlan County, Kentucky, the news spread slowly. But more recently, when there were disturbances in Selma, the news spread instantly. When there were shootings of civilians in Vietnam and this was made known, the news spread instantly. Any disaster anywhere, Peru, Greece, wherever else, we know it. The news pours in. And in the course of this, the basic trust of man in Mother Earth has gone. There is no Noah's Ark to take us out of the flood. What the economist Kenneth Boulding calls Spaceship Earth may not hold us all as population grows and resources dwindle.

Some scientists and engineers have responded to this situation by affirming their belief that we need more science and engineering in order to help us out of these dilemmas. Their basic faith in knowledge has not been shattered; they see more knowledge and more careful application as the cure for past mindless applications of science and technology. I myself am not so sanguine. I share the belief that science and technology may help, but I am not so sure that they will in fact help. However, since I never had an extravagant faith in science, I am not in the position of many students and faculty in the sciences and engineering who, now that their unthinking faith has been shattered, have replaced it by an apocalyptic despair about the future.

One result is a paradoxical alliance between members of the avant-garde who consider science anti-humane and who are intellectual opponents of rationality, and the traditional anti-intellectual American rearguard which wonders what use it is to know how grass grows green. The latter outlook reflects what has been a specifically American and especially male attitude toward bookishness as not being quite manly—an attitude which tended to diminish in the immediate post-World-War-II years, but now again seems to me to be rising. The Gentleman's C was a legacy of that outlook: the idea that a gentleman does not get a better grade than a C except by accident, but coasts through the institution gracefully.

The Gentleman's C might be thought of as a symbol of an older, now vanishing treaty of mutual noninterference between "collegiate" students and more or less scholarly faculty that one could find at many state universities and leading private institutions. This tacit arrangement declared that the students will put out a certain amount of effort and that the faculty will pay them in grades commensurate with effort, and that neither will intrude on the privacy or "real work" of the other. The students will offer a kind of Sunday respect for the faculty, accept a certain amount of influence on their ideals, and go on in most cases to pursue careers other than academic. Indeed, twothirds had had their chance but did not get their A.B.

This is one of the treaties or tacit arrangements now breaking down in the increasingly strained circumstances of academic life. The Sunday respect of students for faculty is diminishing. The students want faculty to "give" more; the faculty in turn often expect more of the students. There was a period in the 1960's when a singularly high proportion of Harvard College students went on to graduate schools of arts and sciences, as many as a third. Now the percentage is half that. One reason of course is the change in the draft laws, and another is the change in the job market. But at least as important, in my judgment, is the loss of belief among undergraduates that academic careers are inviting, that they offer a chance to understand and perhaps even to influence events. Under these circumstances, the Gentleman's C has not returned; instead, we have what I might term the anti-Gentleman's B—the higher grade reflecting among other things more relaxed requirements and faculty misgivings as to the legitimacy of our traditional standards.

The tacit treaties between the various disciplines and schools also break down under these new budgetary pressures and under the cultural conflicts in the society as reflected in the university. These treaties once allowed each academic enterprise within a university to operate in a situation of ecumenical rivalry with more-or-less good-natured snobbery in which physics was superior to chemistry and chemistry to sociology and both to commerce, which might in turn look down on home economics, somehow standing lower than factory economics. But today on the more agitated campuses, the new gradient of academic snobbery is based on "relevance" or relative freedom from complicity in the evils of society.

These student attitudes, unevenly shared among many faculty, have led to an attack on the research-oriented faculty member and an insistence that he get back into the classroom and spend his time with the students. In this outlook, the Right and Left are apt to join hands. The Right want the professors to take the unruly students in hand and keep them quiet, while the Left wants the professors to rap with the students in an egalitarian non-competitive relationship. (Both have a nostalgic image of the old-fashioned liberal arts college in which humane professors did no research; but I can assure you from my reading of college histories that this nostalgic picture is rather false and that many of these old-time faculty members were pedants who had very little to give to students who, as I have already suggested, were seldom in college in order to profit from scholarly mentors.) I myself believe that students on the whole do not benefit from being taught exclusively by men who have no other constituency than the young. If adults do not have an audience of some sort in their own generation, then they depend too much on the young, and may either be left high and dry when youthful fashions change, or they may court popularity by imitating the young rather than seeking to challenge and stimulate them. I do not believe that faculty members need to have a constituency exclusively of their *disciplinary* peers. They may have a constituency of those with whom they consult or work in other capacities. And I would not deny that there are scholar-teachers who do not publish or consult but who can sustain themselves by vicarious contact with the world of scholarship and science. I would add that the life of an academic person who has competing constituencies among his students, his colleagues, his committee members, his disciplinary peers is an intricate and often tension-filled one; but I regard this as on the whole a productive tension, and not one to be simplified and not one to be gotten rid of by succumbing to nostalgic fantasies.

Thus, I am above all troubled when I see faculty members losing their faith in science, in research, in scholarship. My own faith in progress has always been muted, not to say skeptical. I have never thought that bigger was necessarily better; indeed, as a student, I was sympathetic to and somewhat influenced by the Southern Agrarians, and I was later law clerk to Supreme Court Justice Louis D. Brandeis who in many ways shared that rather quirky outlook. I am of course aware of the abuses of science and of rationalism. But I still believe that reason is the only guide we have, wavering as it is. I want the universities to prosper as enclaves of reason. If the old Sunday respect is gone, I would like to see a new respect for universities based on a more realistic sense both of their limitations (for I don't believe they can do a great deal to solve our social problems) and of their opportunities. These are opportunities for discovery of the world in all its aspects, inside us and outside us, on and beyond our planet, of our time and place and out of both. A university is a system of connections, fragile and precarious, with other times and places, "irrelevant" topics, long-lost causes, and esoteric preoccupations. In our society, which is too democratic to have formal systems of patronage or nepotism, the universities have become in fact the patrons of high culture. For me, that high culture includes science and the applied arts and sciences. They help us make our lives more intense, more responsive, and even responsible, even if they do little in the immediate future to help the civic causes we care about or to solve the problems that beset us on all sides. Perhaps it is only something of an overstatement to say that they are essential luxuries.

Let me stop at this point to allow a seventh inning stretch so that anyone who wants to break out of here before we go on for questions can do so.

I know in a hall this size, it's not easy to ask questions, but I'm very patient and I'm sure that in due course people will have questions and comments. Who would like to begin?

Question: What do you see in the future of higher education and how will this development proceed?

DR: I'm not sanguine about this, as I think you might have gathered from my tone. I think that we're in for very, very hard times. Take for example the extent to which what Christopher Jencks and I said about the future of the community colleges has been proved wrong. We thought that these colleges would survive even if the major universities were in difficulty. But it turns out that as bond issues are voted down and taxes are not voted, all public post-secondary institutions in a state may suffer. We have seen a widespread feeling on the part of adults that they don't want to subsidize the education of the young beyond high school and, even in many cases, in the public schools.

Jencks and I have maintained for some years that adult support for higher education is not likely to be sustained unless some of the burden of costs can be shifted on to the young themselves. The strategy we have favored is that proposed by a White House educational panel which has come to be called The Educational Opportunity Bank. Under this scheme, young people would be able to borrow a substantial part of the cost of their higher education, and then to pay it back over something like forty years as a fraction of their regular income tax. This means that if you strike it rich, as a physicist or a sociologist, you will pay back more than if you strike it poor as a social worker or an Assembly of God minister. The problem of women and what can be called "negative dowries" is serious, but not insurmountable, and I think women would benefit from this plan because often their parents don't consider it worthwhile to send them as far or to as good schools as the menfolk in a family that can't affort to do well by all its children. The Educational Opportunity Bank idea seems to me a way to diminish in some measure the feeling of many adults that they are subsidizing the ungrateful young who are getting out of hard work by going to college.

But there are other reasons to support such a proposal. It might make a bit more difficult the maintenance of the present tariffs among the states, which means for example that if you live in Auburn and want to go to Georgia Tech, you have to pay often quite high out-of-state tuition. Similarly, if you are from Atlanta and want to come to Auburn, it is the same story. Moreover, the state universities, although they have had pride in their low tuitions that make them available to all comers, can generally be attended only by the relatively well-off because the universities do not pay subsistence or income foregone. For example, the University of California at Santa Cruz, which is one of the newest and the most sought-after of the California State universities, is said to have a student body whose average family is higher than that of Stanford or Harvard students; for while the students who attend Santa Cruz pay very little tuition, they have to pay for their living expenses at a residential university. At present, the more selective and heavily endowed Harvard University can recruit not only some of the very rich and some of the very poor but some in between because in effect the past and the present rich can help subsidize not only the tuition but the other costs of students from lower income families. I favor The Educational Opportunity Bank, although it is far from a panacea for either the financial or the other troubles of the universities, because it would do that prospectively. It would end up in effect taxing those who became well-off so that they could help subsidize the interest rate and the administrative costs of a system that seems to me only fully workable if it is done on a national basis.

And there would be other advantages. If young people were encouraged to bet on themselves—they would never pay the full cost of their education but only part of it—we might escape some of our present feeling of dependency on the part of students. They would be able to become better customers of higher education and to go where they prefer rather than having to go nearby because it is cheap.

None of this, however, responds in a fundamental way to the fundamental questions I raised concerning the loss of faith in progress and in science, and the consequences of this. And I wonder to what extent here at Auburn one finds the belief that is growing among elite college students that the country simply doesn't need more production, that the Gross National Product is a curse rather than a blessing.

This loss of faith is not being replaced by another faith. It has been replaced by despair, by bursts of instant mysticism, by a feeling that one is humane if one attacks science, which I deeply resent, and by the feeling that the cultural revolution represents some new state of being in mankind. But the trouble with the cultural revolution is that one can't sustain a population of 200,000,000 on the basis of an antiscientific, anti-technological outlook. Part of our problem is to maintain our faith in reason, and in the possibilities of science and technology, while giving up our naive faith in progress. Part of our problem is to maintain a faith in mankind without being starry-eyed. I'm very uncertain about the future in all these respects, but I suppose I am a short-run pessimist and a long-run optimist. My deepest concern since 1945—since Hiroshima—has been about the possibility of the destruction of life by nuclear weapons. This is something new in history, and some of our present misgivings about progress in science and technology reflect that fact. But I feel that if we can manage to control the atom, the weapons of mass destruction, then the serious problems of population and pollution can also be tackled, and we can go on with the human enterprise for the long-run.

Question: What is your opinion about trustees and others such as legislators running the campus, who are not teachers?

DR: Happily, my view on that is not so "subversive" as to make life even harder for President Philpott. Because I think that in the American scheme of things, there is no possibility of a self-sustaining academic enterprise. Many students and faculty members would like to see a totally autonomous university which is nevertheless sustained by the resources of a larger society but not tied to that society by any bond of non-academics (such as trustees or legislators). This ideal of many American faculties is based on looking to European universities which are often more buffered against the public than ours. I think what matters very much are the specific arrangements in specific institutions and such questions as this: Will the trustees feel that they have a responsibility to protect the institution against its outside critics? Do they come to its aid or are they a lightning rod representing the outside to the inside in an unmediated way? It matters here very much whether they are elected on a platform, as in Colorado or in Illinois; whether they run against the university on a platform, let's say, of firing the president or getting rid of all the "bad children." Or whether they're appointed and for what length of term. But what matters also is the culture of the state and whether it has any patrician elite who consider it their job to see that teachers don't get pushed around in their state. Here what has been impressive to me in some Southern universities is the patrician tradition which has protected, for example, the University of Virginia, which one might term a private institution at public expense in Charlottesville. The patrician elite can put up with what the mass public might consider threatening. Similarly, to some degree the University of North Carolina with its branches at Chapel Hill, Greensboro, and Raleigh could draw on this kind of support. I once asked an administrator whether it wasn't an overwhelming job to have, as he did, something like a hundred trustees. He said this meant a lot of dinner parties for the President, but it also meant that if three or four attacked the University of North Carolina, many of the rest—most of them alumni—would come to the University's defense. It also matters very much vis-à-vis legislators and trustees whether an institution has a law school which has trained many of them. I have thought about this in connection with Auburn versus Tuscaloosa: you don't have a law school and you don't have a medical school, but you do have the Agricultural Extension Agents, and you have engineers. I have sometimes asked myself in Michigan whether the lawyers in the legislature, many trained at the University of Michigan, have more power than the county agents, many of them tied to Michigan State University.

In my judgment, this is the kind of issue on which the question turns; many students and faculty are innocent in believing that if there were academics on the board or students on the board, they would be able to act toward the institution in a more protective way. What one needs on the board are people who, as they might say, feel that it's *their* state, *their* university; perhaps they themselves are alumni or their children are; and they are not going to allow anybody to damage the institution.

Now of course this protectiveness can have a two-edged quality. Through the pages of the *Daily Texan*, I have been following the fascinating fight at the University of Texas in Austin between the Chairman of the Board of Regents, Frank Erwin, and many students and faculty at the University to whose interests, as he defines them, he has devoted much of his life. It's his toy in a sense. Apparently, he wants unrestricted admissions; perhaps he is something of a Populist. People in the University want to restrict admissions—it already seems cancerous in size to me—and between him and "his" institution there is thus a cleavage. Even within the same region of the country, there are enormous differences. And even when the governor of the state appoints regents, rather than their being elected, there are still great differences as to how a particular institution fares. Fully to answer your question, one would have to know a great deal about the local landscape.

Question: Is it feasible economically, academically desirable to have post-secondary education for everybody?

DR: Let me recommend an article which has just come out in the current issue of *Fortune* by Edmond K. Faltermayer on just this topic—it's really, I think, quite good. Among other things, it discusses The Educational Opportunity Bank, and suggests in a thoughtful way that everybody ought to get some kind of G. I. Bill of Rights—Bill of Educational Rights—on graduation from high school; with this, people could take out loans (again, repayable through income tax) which they could make use of at any time. I think there's a great deal to be said for people waiting after high school before college, a great deal to be said for putting more weight on adult education and having fewer people come to college when they are 18 or 19. As a teacher, I think it makes a great difference to have a diverse age group in a class. I have heard many students in selective colleges complain, for example, that they are homogeneous because they are all white, suburban, upper middle class, and agreeably affluent; I can't remember hearing them say that they belonged to a single age-grade. That is a far greater homogeneity.

In order to reduce the pressure on people to attend college, there has to be a change in business practice. For what has happened in the last few decades is that businessmen have been able to afford college graduates for jobs that didn't really require a college education. An advertising agency will have a Vassar girl as receptionist because they can afford that prestige: and she's going to be a pretty unhappy receptionist—probably she majored in English, rather than in something sensible for a girl, like science. The article in *Fortune* suggests that business should concern itself with the nature of the work and that then there would be less compulsion on young people to attend a particular kind of institution at a particular time for their post-secondary education.

To turn to another aspect of your question, I believe it is possible to do a great deal more through technical programs at the post secondary level than is now being done. If one concentrates on the concerns of a particular student body and what it comes to the institution with, rather than with what has been traditional in college education; some commuter colleges have sought to see what could be done with "first generation" college students whose parents did not bring them up in cultivated homes. If one focused more on this category of students and what was potentially available to them occupationally and culturally, one might expand the diversity that now exists in post-secondary education.

But to go back to my answer to the first question,

the United States presently faces a real problem as to how to share resources between elite education and popular education; between the education that has created in America a remarkable number of world-class universities and that which has created a remarkable number of institutions that might be thought of as post-secondary high schools at the thirteenth and fourteenth grades, with a high drop-out rate—maybe as much as 50%—even in those years. During the 1950's and 60's we managed in a very uneven way to increase both quantity and quality, both education at the very highest level and education at the mass or popular level. But now with shrinking resources, it seems to me much more difficult to do both things at once. And it is here, as I have already suggested, the major universities may suffer even more than the community colleges do because their expensive programs—their graduate and professional programs—would be especially hard hit when the available resources must be spread more thinly. How to keep heights of scholarship going, let us say astronomy, while also providing greater opportunities for students to come to college, as is now happening in New York City, when they are reading at the eighth-grade level—how to do both these things, I just don't know.

Question: (Inaudible)

DR: Your question touches on the relations between the community colleges and the major research-oriented universities. The California Master Plan was an effort put into effect in 1959 to deal with the problem I just mentioned. The idea was to protect the University of California and what are now its nine campuses from the encroachment of open admissions by creating a community college in virtually every legislative district. The community college would accept people who were either 18 years old or who had completed high school. These colleges could in effect serve as the lower division branches of the University system, and to a lesser degree of the State College system. Indeed, in this somewhat "colonial" relation, the University of California would take transfer students from the community colleges who often did better in their upper-division years at the University than did the regular students who had gone for their freshman and sophomore years to the University. Perhaps the community colleges had smaller classes and more dedicated teachers, or it may have been only the fact that the elect survived and only these transferred.

This system is breaking down. It's breaking down because the University can no longer afford to be so snobbish; it's breaking down because the community colleges tend to focus on their minority of transfer students and not on the great majority. But this is built into the whole social structure and is not really the fault of the community colleges. It is the fault, so to speak, of the feeling of people in America as to what job is appropriate for them. Let me give you an example. I have a friend who teaches English at Los Angeles City College. A Mississippi-born black student comes, he's 18, he's not even finished grade school; at the community college he has a certain number of tests and comes to a counsellor who says to him: "Well, your verbal scores aren't very high, but you have fine manual skills. You should go into the ceramics program. There's a tremendous need for ceramics people; for gifted people in this area." And the black man says: "What do you think, I don't go to Tuskegee to learn to be a Pullman porter, I come here to go to the University. You're putting me down." That's not only a black reaction, although it's now a common black reaction—the white reaction too as to what is a fitting career or life-style that dictates the fitting educational program.

I've talked to a number of Harvard undergraduates in the last few years who, as they put it, reject the rat-race; they want to live naturally, humanly, and they are willing to be handymen on a commune in Vermont. They become carpenters, craftsmen, make sandals and candles. But I have yet to see my first plumber. It's hard to break into plumbing, but it may also be snobbery, covered over by the anti-elitist outlook. What I am suggesting is that the community colleges have problems of status which are not unique to the academic system but reflect the general social system in considerable measure. Many students, sometimes the majority, want the transfer programs rather than the technical programs, and a good many develop neither technical nor academic skills as a result. The college itself finds it difficult to focus on the minority who have clear vocational goals and to develop the technical programs that can respond to these.

Perhaps your question is also related to the Florida pattern of developing upper division universities, such as Florida Atlantic University, designed precisely to take people who have graduated from the community colleges. I have visited Florida Atlantic, and I am very interested in that arrangement. Yet again, its difficulties reflect in part the American style. In the

United Kingdom and I suppose in most countries, one enters a university in a particular program, and if one changes what here would be called a major, one may have to start all over again as a freshman and even apply again as a freshman. One could for example be in a science program at a university and want to transfer to an arts program, and not be able to do that. In the United States, such restrictions on movement do not exist. Hence, a student will come to Florida Atlantic from a community college, let us say he enters in English and decides that instead he wants political science in which he has had no training at all; he will have to start from scratch, and rather than being sent back to the community college, Florida Atlantic will have to lower the ladder so as to prepare a remedial program in political science, while its faculty have come there with the promise of teaching upper-division and graduate students. There *are* problems, but I think we should have more experiments like Florida Atlantic; we should have more experiments with a mix in which people start in one place and end in another, in which one would assume there would be more transfers and more changes—it doesn't fully answer the question.

Question: Yes, What is happening to the curriculum (rest inaudible) . . .?

DR: I think that is a good but also very difficult question. I would say that one curricular change which is happening almost everywhere is the attack on requirements. And in order to say what my own reaction is to these changes requires my saying something about what my own educational ideal is. And when

I have answered this one, I'll call another seventh inning stretch and people can go, and we'll go on with those who want to remain.

What I would like in higher education is to see that people's capacities are stretched. And I suggest that this can be done in the following way: on the one hand they come in to college and are allowed to go on doing well what they have done well in secondary school, but on the other they are also encouraged and if need be forced to do well in something that they have not done or done not very well in secondary school. Most people come to college presenting, so to speak, their best profile—that is the way they define themselves. I think they need to go on doing that in order to have high morale and a sense of competence while they move in another direction. I see this sometimes in terms of the "two cultures" of the sciences and mathematics on the one side and the humanities and the softer social sciences on the other side. (Economics and the harder sorts of psychology would be with the sciences in this respect.) So I see young people coming to college who have been on only one side of that divide and I'd like to see them cross to the other and see that they are sustained through that difficult passage. I'd like to see them expand in another way: deprovincialize whatever their province is—all of us come with a province. And the one I fear most now is the American province—the growing domestication of the United States which reflects the mounting disenchantment between us and the rest of the world. At the same time, we are obsessed with our domestic problems. Some students feel it even illegitimate to have curiosity about some part of the world which is not involved with the race question or American militarism or with our other domestic preoccupations.

Correspondingly, students everywhere want to get rid of language requirements—that's universal—and they say to me when they argue this that we don't really *learn* French, we don't really *learn* German, we don't even really *learn* Spanish. I say yes I agree we don't, but you should demand of your university that it put on an immersion program comparable to that of the Peace Corps, in which you won't be allowed even to swear or make love in English any more, in which you will be exposed to the popular and the high culture of the other country until you are really fluent and you *live* in that other world. Perhaps you will visit it; perhaps this will be done here at home, depending on what you can afford and what the institution can afford. I don't find students on the whole accepting that, and that's what troubles me about what is happening with curricular change.

What is good, what is benign that I see happening also is a greater concern with undergraduate education everywhere, a greater feeling on the part of senior academicians of having to consider what the young are interested in, even if only in order to lead them to what they themselves are interested in. I see a good deal of growth of interdepartmental programs and courses, and I see this on two levels: at the best they transcend the way in which departments have traditionally divided up, somewhat like nations, with rather pointless boundaries; at their worst the interdepartmental programs are ways in which people without any discipline can consider themselves superior to all disciplines.

I would say one thing that I would hope for from higher education in addition to what I have said just now. I would hope that the college years would be a time when young people could be relatively free of guilt: a time in which black students wouldn't feel that they had to be race men—they could be medievalists or anything else that interested them; a time when privileged white students could study astronomy and not feel that it's a luxury and that they ought to be doing something about the ghetto or something about the war. I say this obviously not because I am unconcerned with these problems, but because I feel we are still a rich society in spite of all our troubles and that we can afford, so to speak, to release some young people who may feel an overdose of guilt from the imposition of social and peer pressure—of course the great majority don't feel this pressure at all of taking on themselves the burdens of the society or of the whole world. [Another break was taken.]

DR: I would like to begin this session by saying that I know women have in general softer voices, and on the whole not only here at Auburn but in the nation as a whole, they tend to be less assertive. But I'd be grateful if in the course of this next session which won't go on too long, if some young woman or not so young would feel moved to ask a question.
Question: (Inaudible)
DR: The question begins with the reference to the Report of the Scranton Commission and its discussion of the National Guard at Kent State and Jackson State in contrast to the reaction of the local communities. The students at Kent State were indicted while the

National Guard was exonerated, and the question concerns the effect of these reactions and these controversies on the universities as this is reflected in attitudes and policies toward students. Let me say in the first place that I speak as a friend and admirer of Governor Scranton and that I know some of the people who worked on the staff. Considering all the vicissitudes and all the conflicts within the Commission and between the Commission and its staff, the Report is a remarkable document. It's uneven; I don't think the section on the black colleges is at quite the level of the discussion of the youth revolution in the world as a whole, which is one of the most observant to be found anywhere. So in the first place, I would hope people would read the Report itself and not read only about the Report, and especially in universities I think it would be fruitful reading.

As to the local issue, I would say that the impression I have of the community surrounding Kent State is that it reflects the adult backlash and it is very powerful. Many said that they should have shot more of the students. But as to the young Guardsmen who went to the campus, while I think they may have represented that mood of backlash in a few cases, I think it more important that these were frightened young people in a situation for which they were totally unprepared.

My own feeling has been for a great many years, long before campus disturbances, that we ought to have non-lethal weapons. I'm against guns and for gas. Few other academicians I know of are *for* gas; they are against guns *and* gas, and that's an impossible situation politically and in every other way. If one is going to disarm American police (and we are not

55

in the situation of the United Kingdom: we are an anarchic and violent society and we always have been), then we have to do something else. I'm for the development of a crash research program on non-lethal weapons. But in the absence of that, I think we have also to disarm the students and the radicals. I have signed many "stop the bombing" ads vis-à-vis the bombing of Viet Nam, and a few weeks ago with some pacifist friends we wanted to issue a "stop the bombing" ad for the tiny minority of the terrorist Left. Possibly the terrorists have begun to lose their small following. Of course I don't like it when police kill, beat, or otherwise harass students, or indeed when anybody is savagely treated.

More generally, I think we have to de-escalate our feelings about our political opponents and the symbols we use in attacking them. I've talked with students about this and tried to give them a sense of what is really a class conflict in which they're engaged, often without knowing it. Students on a campus like mine who attack police, scare them; they don't know that they scare them—they feel powerless, the students —they don't realize that the police also feel powerless and frightened often; and are inexperienced. I am not talking about white police or sheriffs versus black students; I'm talking about Northern situations. I am talking about colleges where the students come from the upper middle class and consider themselves cultivated, but behave like hoods in dealing with lower-level civil servants and lower-middle-class people. They are like some aristocrats who have had a romance with peasants but not with "ordinary" middle class people. Consider the movie *The Graduate,* said to be the most popular movie ever in American history; probably most of you saw it—could I have a show of hands if you saw it—yes, probably most of you. Consider the way in which the hero not only dismisses the adults who want to offer him a career in plastics, (although he pollutes the environment with his Porsche and no doubt, while attacking vulgar materialism, has a hi fi set which is expensive, and thousands of dollars of records). But he pushes aside a medical student because he's a square, and beats the medical student to the girl in the end. Well, I think that this is a class conflict really—a kind of class conflict between the affluent lazy and the hard-working middle class. And that conflict is involved in the present political climate, and in the relations between the minority of radical Kent State students and the majority of young people.

And here I think it's important to recognize the enormous gap that separates students and non-students of the same age. In 1968, young people in the North who were not in college voted more heavily for George Wallace than their parents did. And in supporting Wallace when their parents were, in the blue-collar strata, voting on the whole for Humphrey, they were in a way more idealistic as well as more tough than their parents, more expressive, more provocative, less willing to compromise with ordinary standards. They were saying that if their parents' views about disorder, about unruly affluent college students, were right, then George Wallace was the right choice. They were not worried about a depression as their parents were, so that they supported Wallace which was an ideological, hence luxury choice. Similarly, in 1968, many young college students supported Eugene McCarthy or

57

Robert Kennedy much more than did their parents who might have been for Nixon or Humphrey; that is, here also in another context the young people vis-à-vis their parents were similarly ideological and idealistic, similarly provocative. This is the kind of conflict that I think occurs when you have Guardsmen and affluent students: the Guardsmen see the students as having the opportunity at college that they didn't have, as having a good time, and as derogating the very values of study and hard work which would justify their privilege. I don't see this intense cultural conflict as diminishing.

Question: Can you eliminate the class conflict without eliminating classes?

DR: I don't think that you can eliminate class conflict, but I think one can try to moderate its extravagance, and the degree to which the interests of a class are sacrificed to extravagant symbolism. Caring as I do to end the war, I argued with students who were planning to demonstrate last Saturday that their demonstration would help pro-war candidates running against anti-war candidates. If the interest of the students is in ending the war, that kind of conflict does not help their interest. What we see happening in America is a series of righteous symbolic crusades on both sides of a class line, crusades which do not reflect the actual class interests. I believe that each of the conflicting groups has to live with the others, that we have to carry on the conflict by the ordinary democratic means of democratic party struggles.

Question: Do you think there should be any restriction (parietal regulations) in student dormitories? (laughter—something inaudible).

DR: The question is one familiar to me from *The Plainsman;* namely, whether the remaining restrictions existing at colleges are feasible today in terms of the social life of the young; whether the college can serve as a substitute parent. I have a view on this which is somewhat heretical among faculty at elite private colleges. A couple of years ago my colleague John Kenneth Galbraith wrote a letter to the Harvard *Crimson* which got into the national media, in which he declared that it was ridiculous for Harvard to supervise the morals and social behavior of the young; their parents shouldn't send them to Harvard if they were anxious. It was the business of the faculty to teach them and not to monitor how they carried on either their pharmaceutical or love life. This was cheered widely by both students and faculty as you might imagine. I regarded the letter as expressing indifference, and felt that it did not take account of real problems for which the usual supervisory rules are no answer, but for which I want to look for other answers.

Let me illustrate what I mean. Two years ago, I was asked by a Harvard freshman proctor to come and meet with his thirty freshmen advisees. He had a table in the Freshman Union, a private room off the main noisy place, and as we were eating, he said, turning to the students, I guess you've all tried pot. Now I could see immediately what was on *his* mind. He was a very square young law student who wanted to say to the freshmen that he was on their side and that he wasn't somebody to whom they couldn't bring their personal problems; he would understand. But I stopped him immediately, and said "You've just done a terrible thing. You've increased the already enormous peer pressure to have tried pot; your assumption makes it more difficult to refrain." Then I continued, turning to the freshmen and said: "I wonder if there is anybody in this room, in this group of young men, so foolhardy, so quixotic to admit that he hasn't tried pot?" One hand shyly went up; another went up; finally 30% of the hands were up. And I turned to the proctor and I said that he had innocently been helping create a self-confirming prophecy that everybody tries pot. On many campuses today, the belief is widespread that anybody who is a virgin is hung up on frigidity.

The peer pressure is formidable. And if adults remove all supervision, that pressure takes over. What does one do about it? If one is compassionate, concerned, and interested in allowing the young to mature at their own time and rate, I don't know the answer. I do believe that there should be an "age of consent" in both politics and culture; I'm against politicizing the seventh grade, whereas a number of my own college students are trying to mobilize the seventh grade.

Again, I don't know the answer. One possibility is to arrange for meetings of small groups of freshmen with older people, perhaps on a single-sex basis. When I suggested a few years ago to President Bunting of Radcliffe that we have such discussion with Radcliffe students alone, she thought I was very square; that boys and girls could now talk with utter candor in each other's presence. But I think that is not true. I think there is a considerable difference in the forms single-sex discussions of certain issues take, especially in the case of the coed when the campus is in style masculine and where the values are masculine.

I think girls need to learn how to manage academically and humanly in such a male environment; also many boys are shy, and they need some single-sex situations, not necessarily to talk about sex at all, but about anything. One has to find substitutes for the old rules, substitutes which would vary from locale to locale, and which I do not see adequately provided anywhere.

Question: How do you feel about the activism today in sociology among young sociologists?

DR: I want to do something very hard, which is to compartmentalize in some measure the life of the university and the life of the society. At the sociology meetings in September, I talked on just this issue. I argued with some of my fellow sociologists that the precinct in which they should be active is the regular political precinct and not the college. Some answered me and said: "The college is the precinct we know best and where we can make the greatest change." My reaction to that was that this was an indolent judgment. The only real precinct is the regular one outside the campus. Activity there may of course not always be successful, but that's no reason not to keep trying; of course there will be different luck in politics in different parts of the country.

And when I speak of a precinct, I'm not speaking only of lobbying for individual votes among the voters, but of working with the clergy, working with the newspapers, working with alumni, seeking to influence one's own parents, and getting students to do the same: developing a network where one can have some influence and even success.

I know that on this subject I'm probably in the minority among sociologists. The distinctions I want to make are difficult and subtle; let me illustrate. In 1967 at the San Francisco sociology meetings, there was a move by the radical activists to have the Sociological Association go on record against the Viet Nam war. While I had been opposed to the war since 1954, I was one of those who helped draft the statement that was circulated by mail to all the sociologists in the country which allowed them to go on record against the war as individuals. I was opposed to a resolution at a meeting which would bind the Association by a caucus of a minority. It is possible indeed that a secret ballot might have had a different result even in the San Francisco of 1967 for I imagine something like 95% of American sociologists are against the war, as 92% of the philosophers would be, and the overwhelming majority of academics generally today. This kind of distinction between the Association as a body and individuals acting as individuals is the kind of distinction that I make and which many activists consider meaningless, beside the point while people are dying.

What keeps me on my more complicated course is the belief that one has to act at every moment as if the society is going to be better rather than worse, even if one in fact thinks it is going to be worse, as at the moment I do. This attitude of mine is perhaps a fundamentally religious one. In other words, one has to try in one's own environment to act in a way which is non-polemical, non-violent, non-despairing, hopeful even without hope, faithful even without faith, skeptical but not cynical; and go on that way.

My feeling about many of the radical activists in sociology is that they are not able to have more than a single interest. I think mankind does not go on with only a single interest. I've indicated already my passionate and abiding concern about nuclear weaponry. My feeling since Hiroshima is that this is the most important issue facing the human race—the possibility of extinction. And I don't think we can put that issue aside although we've had good luck so far. For I care about the SALT talks in Helsinki and Vienna and follow them with deep concern; care about this even more than about the Viet Nam war. I care about the war in part because I continue to feel that it may escalate; after all, the President wanted to drop nuclear bombs on Dinh Bien Phu in 1954 when he was Vice-President. Feeling that way, nevertheless, if I thought about nothing else, if I were *only* an activist, I would feel I would be sterile, fanatical, and quickly exhausted as so many of the activists are quickly exhausted. Because I can think about poetry and astronomy and many other things, I may be able to keep my sanity and be perhaps more effective in attacking the dangers of nuclear weapons, and even face the realities and dangers perhaps a bit better.

Walter W. Heller

Economic Growth
and the Quality and Equality of Life

Walter W. Heller

Economic Growth
and the Quality and Equality of Life

IN THIS ERA OF QUESTIONING AND DISCONTENT, one
of the prime objects of challenge and reexamination,
especially by the young, is Economic Growth. It is
fair to say, I believe, that from a period when people
thronged to the temple of economic growth, eager for
its blessings and largely blind to its curses, we have
swung toward an age of doubt and disbelief in the
virtues, and rising resentment against the vices, of
economic growth. Increasingly, the young want to tear
down the temple of growth—witness the drive for zero
economic growth; or at least drive the money changers
from the temple—witness the calls for drastic redistribution of income and wealth.

In part, youth's disenchantment with growth arises
from the realization that their elders have achieved
abundance without happiness. The great rise in GNP
in recent decades—especially in the 1960's, when real
income per family (in constant dollars) rose nearly 40%
—has not brought about the personal gratification, the

better life, the remedies of social injustices that should have come with such material advances. They see that growth is not synonymous with social progress, that even a full-time job and a decent income are not synonymous with the good life and personal contentment. And they see that as a nation, great wealth—the greatest any nation has ever known—has not been translated into a great society.

Coupled with this vague sense that the pursuit of growth is not tantamount to—and may even be antithetical to—the pursuit of happiness is the rising alarm over the environmental costs of growth, the growing belief that growth of population and production are destroying not only the quality of our environment, but the resource base and eco-system essential to life itself. It is small wonder that growthmen have been put on the defensive.

Indeed, in the atmosphere on the campus today, I know that in making even a qualified defense of growth, I run the risk of being labelled a growth-maniac or perhaps the Abominable Growthman. Yet, I do rise to that qualified defense. I seek a middle ground, a position that on one hand recognizes the environmental havoc and social defects of growth and points ways to minimize its costs, but on the other defends growth as a basic ingredient of social progress and political stability in a free society, as ingredient for which no substitute has yet been found.

To hold my examination of the vast subject of growth and the quality and equality of life within bounds, I will focus on three main aspects of the problem: ——first, a rather searching probe into the interaction of growth and environmental deterioration;

——second, and more briefly, the interplay between growth, poverty, and equality;

——third, the role that a "new economic consciousness" might play in redirecting growth into less polluting and more fulfilling channels.

Growth and the Environment[1]

The conflict between ecologists and economists, between neo-Malthusians and defenders of growth, has become more and more sharply drawn. In starkest terms, the ecologist or neo-Malthusian confronts us with an environmental imperative that requires zero economic growth—a sharp curtailment today and an end to economic growth tomorrow—as the price of biological survival. In contrast, the economist or growth-defender counters with a socioeconomic imperative that requires the continuation of growth as the price of social survival. Some ecologists see the arresting of growth as a necessary, though not sufficient, condition for saving the eco-system. The economist sees growth as a necessary, though not sufficient, condition for social progress and stability. He tends to regard the structure rather than the fact of growth as the main root of environmental evil and, indeed, doubts that the resources, revenues, and institutional changes required to restore the environment will be forthcoming in the absence of growth.

Before joining the issue, a further word about the recent alarums sounded by the Club of Rome and by Meadows and Forrester (notably in *The Limits to Growth*), about their position that growth is self terminating or self-destructive. Their position boils down to this: Resources are finite, so growth cannot be infinite. The supply of air, water, land, and minerals in the earth's skin is fixed by nature, so man had better adapt himself to those fixed limits by limiting, indeed stopping, population growth and economic growth.

Let me note in passing that, without knowing whether Meadows and Forrester are right or wrong, I have a good deal of sympathy for the population side of their formula. Zero Population Growth fixes our attention where it belongs, namely, on per capita growth, per capita quality and well-being in life. It is the physical and psychic well-being of the individual that counts, and unlimited population growth would put that well-being in jeopardy on both counts.

But to return to the deceptively simple logic of the Meadows and Forrester model. Not only is the "magnificent dynamics" of that model under serious question and attack—i.e., not only is their model deficient and incomplete, and their theory unverified—but suppose we were to accept their imperatives amd conclude that growth must eventually be checked or stopped. Would this in any way conflict with the search for ways and means of making growth (or simply production) less costly and detrimental to the environment and of redirecting growth to more beneficial uses? No—that search is all the more important since, however strong the case against growth may prove to be, the combination of political courage and economic skill needed to stop it does not yet exist. Whatever the eventual outcome of the escalating controversy over *The Limits to Growth,* no one will quarrel with the urgency of the need to de-fang growth, to rid it so far as possible of its propensity to poison the environment. Nor need the controversy interfere with the fairer sharing of the proceeds of growth and production. As someone has observed, all the talk of stop-the-world-I-want-to-get-off must have a pretty hollow ring to the poor and the non-white not only in America, but throughout the less developed world—who have never had a chance to climb on!

As we tackle this issue of growth-versus-environment, we have to keep in mind that the contest between the two is in one sense a mismatch: Economic growth is a means, an instrumental goal, while environmental quality is an end in itself, an important component of the quality of existence. Let me underscore that in words I used in a speech in 1961:

> There is a Viennese joke to the effect that psycho-analysis is the disease of which it purports to be the cure. Economic growth is not like that. It is not itself a social goal in the ultimate sense in which we are using the word. But economic growth is a most important element in permitting our country to achieve its national goals.

With this prologue, we turn directly to the tough questions about growth:

- Is it growth itself, or only particular forms of growth, particular technologies, particular uses of resources, that damage the environment?
- What would be the real costs in social terms to arrest growth?
- Could there even, as a practical matter, *be* a successful war on pollution without growth?

Such questions imply that we have a realistic option of stopping growth, or at least slowing it down to what ecologists might regard a comfortable crawl. But do we? The deepest wellspring of modern economic growth is the advance of knowledge. It is inconceivable that we could quench man's thirst for understanding and throttle his quest for easier ways of doing things. Yet, without these restrictions, the output per man hour invariably rises. We might, of course, hold total output in check by the imposition of highly restrictive taxes and tight monetary policies or of some form of direct public control. Output per man hour, however, would still continue to rise: Therefore, total stoppage of growth would require a rapid decline in the average work week—one calculation puts it at 26 hours by 1980—and a corresponding increase in leisure and nonmarket activity.

A policy of zero population growth would make only a limited contribution to this undertaking. The Chief of the Population Division of the Bureau of Census, Herman P. Miller, has pointed out that "two-thirds of the rise in expenditure for goods and services would take place even if our population stopped growing tomorrow, but continued to increase its income and spend its money in the same old way."

The purpose of a no-growth policy would be to check and reverse the erosion of the environment. But nothing about a no-growth economy would by itself insure an alteration of our present polluting ways. For this, one has to posit rigorous and extremely costly measures to restore and protect the environment, which would in turn require an absolute reduction in our material standards of living.

Just to sketch this picture is to raise serious questions of its social, political, and economic feasibility. Short of a believable threat of human extinction, it is hard to imagine that the public would accept the tight controls, lowered living standards, and large income transfers required to create and manage a stationary state. Whether the necessary shifts could be accomplished without vast unemployment and economic dislocation is another question. Moving on to a basis of no-growth might even throw the after all rather fragile ecology of our economic system so out of kilter as to threaten its breakdown.

Naturally if humanity were to discover that the only alternative to outright suicide was a serious reduction in its standard of living, either actual or aspired to, I dare say we would find some way to manage the economic system so that it could accommodate such a necessity. Short of this most extreme threat, however, economic growth seems destined to continue. Thus our task must be rather to *redirect* growth, to reshape the means and forms through which we are to grow and to reorder our standards of the purposes to be served by growing.

What would benign growth look like? First of all, it is essential to take this question out of the one-dimensional context of the natural environment. In a broader context, the environmental claims against the bounties of growth must include shares not only for cleansing the physical environment of air, water, and land pollution and of urban congestion and sprawl, but also for

———cleansing the social environment of the cancers of poverty, ignorance, malnutrition, and disease.

———cleansing the human environment of the degradation and blight of the urban ghetto and the rural slum.

——cleansing our personal environment of the fear of crime and violence.

Even with the aid of a rise of 55% in GNP and 34% in real per capita personal income from 1959 to 1969, we found that our inroads on these problems did not keep pace with our rising expectations and aspirations. Imagine the tensions between rich and poor, between black and white, between blue-collar and white-collar workers, between old and young, if we had been forced to finance even the minimal demands of the disadvantaged out of a no-growth national income instead of a one-third increase in that income.

A specific example may be instructive. Between 1959 and 1969, the number of persons below the poverty line fell from 39 million to 24 million, from 22.4% to 12.2% of a rising population. That improvement came from a 3% increase in productivity per year, a drop in unemployment from 6% to 4%, shifts of the poor from lower to higher income occupations and regions, and an extraordinary growth in government cash transfers, from $26 billion in 1960 to over $50 billion in 1970. Every one of these factors is in some way the direct outgrowth of, or associated with, or facilitated by, per capita economic growth.[2] Given their huge stake in growth as a source not only of the wherewithal but also as much of the will to improve their lot, the poor could be pardoned for saying "Damn the externalities, full speed ahead."

Looking ahead, the Brookings Institution projects a rise in real GNP (in 1971 dollars) of $350 billion or 34%, from 1971 to 1977. In the face of claims on these increases that are already staked out or clearly in the making—claims that leave only a tiny net "fiscal dividend" by 1977—it will be hard enough to finance the wars on poverty, discrimination, and pollution even *with* vigorous economic growth.[3] Consider the problem in a no-growth setting: to wrench resources away from one use to transplant them in another, to wrest incomes from one group for transfer to another, to redeploy federal revenues from current to new channels (even assuming that we could pry loose a substantial part of the $77 billion devoted annually to military expenditures)—and to do all this on a sufficient scale to meet the urgent social problems that face us—might well plunge us into unbearable social and political turmoil. In this context, one rightly views growth as a necessary condition for social advance, for improving the quality of the *total* environment.

Apart from the tangible bounties that growth can bestow, we should keep in mind some of its intangible dividends. Change, innovation, and risk thrive in an atmosphere of growth. It fosters a social mobility and opens up options that no stationary state can provide. This is not to deny that a no-growth economy, with its large rations of leisure, would appeal to those of you in the upcoming generation who lay less store by the work ethic and material goods than your forebears. But if you associate such a condition with tranquility—in the face of the intensified struggle for shares of a fixed income on the part of your more numerous and more competitive contemporaries—I believe you are deluded.

Let me return now to the context of the strictly natural environment. More and more, we have come to understand that we have to stop and reverse the ugly and destructive waste disposal practices of our modern society. But to accomplish this, we will

——have to call on the taxpayer to foot huge bills both to overcome our past neglect and to finance proper collective waste treatment and preserve open space and wilderness.

——have to ask producers and consumers to bear the brunt of outright bans on ecologically dangerous materials and to pay "rent" for the use of the environment's waste assimilation services—such as our lakes, rivers, and air—that they have been enjoying largely free of charge.

A recent estimate of the demands on the federal budget for its share of an adequate environmental program would triple the present outlay of $6 billion a year to about $18 billion a year, an increase of some $60 billion over the next 5 years. Without growth, and given the limits to the congressional will to tax, how could we hope to raise the required revenues?

The government's share of the cost is only the beginning. Industry and agriculture, and ultimately the consumer, will have to absorb a large part of the costs of saving the environment. Responsible estimates place the total annual cost of achieving current goals in the case of water pollution (secondary treatment) at $40 billion a year by 1980. To achieve the higher standards of clean water (tertiary treatment) and clean air that many now demand would double this figure to $80 billion annually.[4] Compared with the $5 billion or so we were spending for pollution control in 1970, these costs are huge. Indeed, in a stationary state they would be staggering. But a growing economy would cut them to size. Given normal growth, the nation's annual output will be about $550 billion greater in 1980 than in 1970. Devoting only 7% of this increase to pollution control will finance significant improvements in air and water quality. And even if the country were shocked into the all-out $80-billion-a-year program, it could do so by earmarking less than one-sixth of the increase in GNP to the war on pollution.

But imagine the resistance of business and agriculture to absorbing huge anti-pollution costs in a fixed-profit society, let alone the resistance of consumers to bearing their share of the burden in higher prices in a world of fixed incomes. Again, if the only alternative, if the ultimate cost, were biological self-destruction, the answers would be different. But in the absence of that fate, or its extreme remoteness, growth becomes a vital social lubricant, our best bet for getting people to give up private "goods" to overcome public "bads."

To all this, the ecologist and his youthful allies may counter that the Great God Growth has feet of clay. In their view, if we counted the full costs of water, air, land, visual, and noise pollution—that is, the drawing down of our environmental capital—the advance of measured GNP in the past quarter century might well turn out to be an illusion. In responding, the economist is at pains to make clear that he is anything but Mecca-nistic about GNP. He is under no illusion that GNP is an index of social welfare (or, for that matter, that it is even feasible to construct a single index of welfare, or that greater material welfare is any guarantee of greater happiness). But he does believe that a careful reading of economic and social data yields persuasive evidence

——that real GNP per capita *has* advanced even after adjusting for increases in population, prices, and pollution.

——that a rise in social welfare *has* accompanied the rise in output of goods and services.

It should require no lengthy demonstration to show that, while a significant part of GNP is illusory when it comes to social welfare,[5] wide differences and large advances in per capita GNP are undeniably associated with significant differences and advances in wellbeing. Robert Lampman, for instance, found that a 26% gain in real GNP per capita from 1947 to 1962 brought with it a 26% gain in per capita private consumption, a distinct improvement in income security, and a significant reduction in poverty. He concluded: "All things considered, the pattern of growth in the United States in the post-war years yielded benefits to individuals far in excess of the costs it required of them. To that extent, our material progress has had humane content."[6]

Economists labor under no illusion that GNP is a satisfactory measure of welfare or that it can be turned into one. They would readily agree with Petit-Senn that "not what we have, but what we enjoy, constitutes our abundance." What makes people think that GNP has become the economist's Holy Grail is that it has assumed an indispensable role in measuring, first, the economy's output potential and, second, its performance in using that potential.

All observers agree that no amount of adjustment

of the national accounts can capture the myriad values and subtleties that are required to measure social welfare. Indeed, no single index of social welfare can be calculated because we have nothing like the pricing system to solve the impossible problem of attaching weights to the various components, be they pollution, crime, health, discrimination, or whatever. But to conclude that no *single* index can be constructed is not to undermine or discourage the efforts to develop a set of social indicators, not anchored in the GNP accounts, that will permit us to make better judgments on advances as well as failures in social performance.

Coping with the Environmental Threat

Growth *can* be reformed to become less polluting of the biosphere and less profligate in the use of resources. It *can* give us the real and financial wherewithal to mount a massive campaign against environmental pollution and profligacy. But *how?* What changes in economic institutions and incentives are needed? And can they be effected in a political and social milieu of freedom and a market system whose primary guide is self-interest and the profit motive? Or is the path to environmental self-preservation to be found only in a political and ethical revolution that substitutes social for private gain, altruism for selfishness, as the prime movers of human economic activity?

Since that revolution is neither at hand nor in sight, our only available remedy today is self-imposed collective coercion (regulation and taxation) and the harnessing of the profit motive to make pollution costly and anti-pollution profitable. In particular, we need to penalize technology that is environmentally wanton and wasteful, and reward technology that husbands resources and protects the environment.

In seeking practical ways to cope with the environmental threat, reluctance to impose the taxes and regulations needed to serve this end is by no means the only difficulty. There is a prior problem; namely, divergent modes of thought. At the risk of exaggerating a bit for emphasis, I perceive the dedicated environmentalist as thinking in terms of rapidly increasing rates of deterioration, threshholds, flashpoints, and absolute limits to be dealt with by absolute bans. (And I tend to succumb to absolutism myself, I must confess, when it comes to oil exploration in Puget Sound, roads in the North Cascades, and nearly 70,000 tons a day of taconite tailings dumped into Lake Superior.)

In basic approach, the economist could hardly agree less. He thinks in terms of marginalism, trade-offs, a careful cost-benefit calculus. He urges striking a balance between nature and man, between environment and growth, between technology and ecology. The right solution, to an economist, would be one that pushes de-pollution to the point where the costs just equal the benefits. What he seeks is not *maximum* cleansing of the environment (prohibitions tend to be prohibitively expensive) but an *optimum* arising out of a careful matching of the "bads" that are overcome and the "goods" that are foregone in the process.

This leads the economist to pursue the optimum by selecting the right procedures—forcing the producer to bear the full cost and the consumer to pay the full price for waste-disposal access to the environment, thus building anti-pollution incentives into the market process—unlike the ecologist whose instinct is to prescribe the right outcome; namely, ending or drastically curtailing pollution. The economist is also dedicated to this outcome. But he wants the market system, rather than a government regulator, to do as much of the work for him as possible.

For there to be any genuine meeting of minds, the ecologist will have to overcome his natural impatience with concepts of careful balancing of costs and benefits, an impatience that undoubtedly grows out of his feeling that cost-benefit analyses appear to bear too little relation to the moral and ethical issues at stake, that the more or less infinite benefits of environmental preservation make refined cost calculations more or less irrelevant. And for his part, the economist will have to break out of the web of marginal balance where the costs and benefits that truly matter cannot be contained within that web. Irreparable damage—whether to human health by arsenic and lead poisoning, or to bald eagles by DDT, or to the Alaskan tundra by hot oil, or to the beauty of a canyon by a hydro-electric dam—cannot be handled by the fine tuning of marginalism. Nor is the economist's balancing act applicable in cases where the benefits are short-run and calculable while costs are long-run and incalculable. So he must beware of forcing onto the pricing mechanism jobs that it will almost surely do badly. Yet, taking full account of all this, he insists that the cost-benefit principle remains applicable to a very broad range of pollution problems where measurements or reasonable approximations *are* possible.

We are still in the early stages of identifying, quantifying, and countering the multiple threats to our environment. It may be that we are too quick in accepting the concept of finite limits and closing physical frontiers implicit in the concept, dramatized by Kenneth Boulding, of Spaceship Earth. At least two previous episodes in our history come to mind to suggest that we may yet be able to turn the ecological dials back from the "self-destruct" position without stopping growth in output, energy, technology, and living standards.

The first was the closing of America's geographical frontiers, which allegedly robbed this country of much of its mobility and dynamism. But other frontiers—scientific, technological, economic—soon opened up new vistas and opportunities, new frontiers which far surpassed any merely physical ones.

The second episode is much more recent. We do not need to stretch our memories very far to recall the great furor some 20 to 25 years ago about "running out of resources," especially energy, mineral, and other natural resources. We were being told by presidential commissions that we were about to exhaust our supplies of mineral resources and the productive potential of our agricultural land. But as we now know, intensive scientific research and technological development—responding partly to the alarums that were sounded, but mostly to the signals sent out by the pricing system—resulted in the upgrading of old resources, the discovery of new ones, the development of substitutes, and the application of more efficient ways of utilizing available resources.

Today, our most pressing problem is less one of limited resource availability and more one of growing threats to environmental quality and the metabolism

of the biosphere. Concentrations of toxic and nonde-
gradable wastes pose a mounting problem. But at this
relatively early stage of our environmental experience
and awareness, it seems premature to conclude that
mounting problems are insurmountable. As our new
knowledge and concern are translated into changes
in our institutional arrangements and cost-price structure, strong incentives will be generated to redirect
production and technology into less destructive channels.

One can, for instance, conceive of scientific and
technological discoveries that would enable us to
import solar energy, at least for purposes of photo-
synthesis, and perhaps even to build a proxy for the
sun in the form of fusion power, triggered with the
aid of laser beams, sometime in the next half century
or so. One gallon of water might give us the energy
we now get from 7 barrels of crude oil. Electricity
would be penny cheap but no longer pound foolish.
Recycling of wastes would be routine. Reconstituting
of natural resources would come into the realm of the
possible. Conceivably, science could still unlock the
doors that, the ecologist fears, economic growth is closing all around us.

Perhaps the critical point of difference between
economists and ecologists on the certainty of our de-
scent into an environmental hell rests in their sharply
divergent attitudes toward technology. The ecologist
sees pollution-intensive technology at the heart of a
mindless pursuit of economic growth. The economist
points out how often the relation between technological advance and pollution has been, precisely, an
inverse one, as in cases where technology has made

it possible to conserve materials or recycle wastes. This dichotomy runs far deeper than any mere disagreement on facts. For even if we grant the basis in truth of Barry Commoner's view that it is the technology involved in U. S. growth which is destroying our environment, there still remains the critical operational question: Is this technology autonomous and out of control, is it an inevitable concomitant of growth? Or does progress in science and technology respond to social and economic forces? If so, can it be bent to our will?

An affirmative answer to the last two questions is emerging from recent investigations. The direction of technical changes in the private sector as well as the emphasis of research in the public sector are shown to respond to differences in the relative prices of natural resources and other factors of production. It follows that if we assess the right charges for waste disposal and put the right prices on resource amenities, we will not only improve the pattern of production to the benefit of the environment but also stimulate pollution-abating technology. Indeed, this longer-run impact on the direction of technological effort may be considerably more important than the short-run resource allocation effects.

As we make abatement mandatory or painfully costly, the relevant technology will no longer be treated on a band-aid or after-thought basis, an approach that is likely to be inefficient and costly. Instead, it will be done on a preventive, built-in, advanced-planning basis. And as economic growth leads to replacement of old processes, equipment and plants with new ones, it will hasten the change to cleaner and healthier methods of production. In short, if we now put proper prices on air, water, quiet, and landscape, it seems reasonable to assume that the market mechanism will cause new shifts in resource use and technology leading us to conserve these resources and let Spaceship Earth cruise on a good deal longer.

Although ecologists and economists are not likely to agree on precisely how far the battle against pollution should be pushed—on how many social and material "goods" should be given up to overcome environmental "bads"—one perceives some early signs of convergence on the policy approaches and instruments to be used in that battle. They would agree that where the trade-off is between today's "goods" and tomorrow's "bads," government has to step in to enforce a rational calculus. Many environmental problems can be handled only by government prohibitions and regulations (mercury and DDT come to mind) and by public expenditures for collective sewage disposal, land reclamation, and environmental clean-up. They can also join hands in identifying the essentially costless changes that serve growth and the environment simultaneously; for example, converting the heat thrown off in producing energy from a pollutant to a productive source of space heating and cooling for industrial, commercial, and apartment buildings.

But where hard choices will have to be made, as I have already made clear, the economist wants to put as much of the load on the price system as it can efficiently carry. More specifically, his main device would be to put price tags in the form of effluent charges, or emissions taxes, or refundable materials fees on the now largely free use of air, water, and land areas as dumping grounds for industrial and commercial wastes. The environmentalist's instinct is to recoil against this "license to pollute." But even here, we find the great majority of environmental organizations banding together in the Coalition to Tax Pollution, with their first target the enactment of an effective tax on sulfur oxide emissions. The economist says "Right on!" for he wants to spread the net of the pricing mechanism widely to capitalize on its automaticity in digesting information and responding to it, its ability to integrate a vast range of decisions, its stimulus to natural resource conservation, and its lowering of demands on the government bureaucracy. His goal, of course, is not to collect fees or taxes, but to build enough economic incentives into the market system to bring pollution to bay.

Growth, Poverty, and Equality

As we increasingly inject the costs of clean waste disposal and resource conservation into the prices of our products, GNP may not suffer greatly in quantity, but it will change in quality, containing more environmental safeguards and amenities and less material output. Given the high income elasticity of demand for environmental services, the intuitive reaction of most of those who hear or read these lines will be inwardly to smile with satisfaction.

But how will the poor and the black ghetto dwellers view the matter? What do environmental attractions, aesthetics, and amenities mean to them? Perhaps somewhat cleaner air and water, but more pertinently:

————higher prices of the goods that will now bear the costs of producing those three A's.

————little help with what Congressman Rangel from Harlem says "ecology" means to his constituents: "Who's gonna collect the damned garbage?"

So before we take much solace in the improved mix of the national output as *we* see it, before environmentalism takes the élitist path, we had better be sure (a) that the ghetto dweller is cut in on the environmental dividends as *he* sees them and (b) also that as we end industry's free ride on public air and water and land and thereby raise the prices of goods bought by the poor, we simultaneously compensate them through more effective measures to redistribute income and opportunity.

Growth will not automatically do the redistributive job for us. The Great Depression and World War II were effective in reducing inequality—the depression, by putting many of the wealthy through the wringer, and the war, by giving jobs, income, and skills to millions of the poor and disadvantaged. But since the war, the U. S. income distribution has been all but static in the face of unprecedented growth.

Not that social justice, in its economic dimensions, demands complete equality of income and wealth. Abstractly, what it requires, first, is that inequality be reduced to the point where such inequality as remains be to everyone's advantage; that is, where any further reduction in inequality would worsen the position of the least advantaged individual or group, presumably by undermining incentives and the like. And second, it requires upward mobility: that positions of authority, command, and affluence be open to all in society. Economic growth serves the second requirement well. It opens up new options, maintains mobility, and constantly refuels the hope for betterment in a way that the stationary state could never match. Granted, it also heightens the sense of frustration and envy on the part of those who don't make it, those who don't share equitably in the fruits of progress. So we must ask: What is the record of U. S. economic growth in redistributing income and lifting the poor out of their poverty status?

To be precise, in the quarter century since World War II, the combination of growth and legislated social measures has increased the percentage share of total personal income received by the lowest one-fifth of our population by only 15% (from a miserable 4.0% of total income to an only slightly less miserable 4.6% of total income). The income share of the top 5% of our population has been cut by 15% in the same period. But these changes are so miniscule as to support the general statement that the rapid growth of the U. S. economy since the War has altered income distribution very little indeed. We can be sure that the U. S. distribution is still a far cry from the optimum demanded by any reasonable definition of social justice.

Turning from the relative to the absolute impact of growth on the lowest income group, we find a sharply different picture. The reduction of poverty was dramatic. Defining poverty as a $4000 income (in 1970 dollars) for a family of four, we find that the proportion of U. S. families in poverty dropped from 33% in 1947 to 22% in 1959 and 13% in 1969.

Yet, in the face of this vast improvement in material

well-being, reduction of poverty, and decline in hardship—in the face of the sharp growth of welfare in the material sense—there has been a parallel growth of a sense of social malaise, a growing awareness and perception of social injustice. In part, but not by any means entirely, this is associated with the tragic mistake of Viet Nam. But even apart from Viet Nam, it arises from such sociological factors as the civil rights revolution, the youth rebellion, the nationwide explosion of aspirations, and the liberating affect of rising income and a rising education. Growth may be a necessary condition for happiness, but it is surely not sufficient!

A New "Econsciousness"?

To make growth cleaner, more benign, more enjoyable is the immediate task that confronts the nation. We have to go about it at once, without waiting for a "soft revolution" in individual morality and motivation—but also, one might add, without giving up hope that the role of national or collective interest will rise and the role of self-interest will diminish in guiding the actions of individuals and private business. Fortunately, there are signs that our collective or public morality on growth and the environment is changing and, perforce, improving—improving in the sense of a growing willingness to impose collective curbs and penalties on individual actions that foul the environment and misuse resources like air and water that belong to all of us. By reasoned and responsive collective decisions to capitalize on, rather than capitulate to, the stubborn individual morality of self-interest, we can and will cut the costs and boost the benefits of economic growth—make growth less and less an agent of environmental destruction and more and more an effective engine of social justice.

As we pursue the long hard struggle to change individual morality—to achieve a revolution of the spirit—we must in the meanwhile, then, do everything possible to turn self-interest to public interest. The "Prosaic Persuaders"—taxes, charges, and penalties—must be applied to turn the profit motive of the individual to the interest of society.

Some will recoil from this dependence on self-interest and the profit motive. They speak longingly, or even darkly, or an overthrow of existing institutions as the only path to environmental salvation. Others yearn for a world in which everything will be done for love—love not of self, but of one's fellow man. But given a world in which most things are done for individual gain or profit, let's make what is socially harmful unprofitable and what is socially good profitable. If sulfur emissions are contaminating the air around us, let's impose such heavy taxes on each pound of sulfur oxide emitted that it will be more profitable to de-pollute than pay the tax. Reliance on the profit motive? Yes. Pro bono publico? Yes.

To make economic growth not only compatible with, but a servant of, a high-quality environment won't be easy. Even after ecologists identify the source of the trouble, engineers identify solutions and develop monitoring devices, and economists identify appropriate taxing and pricing schemes, there remain crucial tests of public will and political skill. To get producers and consumers to pay the full cost of using the environment for waste disposal and to get the public to accept the reordered priorities and pay the higher taxes that will be needed to redirect growth and clean up past environmental mistakes will require great acts of *both* will and skill.

But it is worth repeating that while this route to the reform of economic growth calls for some change in collective morality—one that is already under way—it does not depend on a revolution in individual morality. Charles Reich, in his *Greening of America* may not persuade us—he has not persuaded me—that a new individual consciousness is sweeping the land. But he raises an intriguing question, one that suggests to me a parallel in economic life and motivation. On reflection, three rather distinct levels of economic consciousness ('Econsciousness' for short) are identifiable, roughly matching Reich's three levels of general consciousness.

Econsciousness I is identified with Adam Smith's "unseen hand," the idea that each person in seeking his self-interest necessarily serves the interests of others. Whether you grow potatoes, shine shoes, or tend a machine to make a living, you are automatically being serviceable to somebody else. Similarly, if you earn interest by saving and lending money, or profit by running a textile mill, you do so only by providing the services or goods someone needs. Guided by the "invisible hand" of self-interest, the free market system neatly serves the national interest. What a comfortable moral code: I gain, therefore I serve!

In fairness to Smith, one should note in passing that the doctrine of the unseen hand has to be understood in terms of the system against which he was rebelling; namely, the 18th century guild system which blanketed the economy with tight wage-price controls. So *The Wealth of Nations* was actually a "declaration of economic independence," published appropriately enough in 1776, paralleling our political Declaration of Independence.

Then came Econsciousness II, which has three sub-stages. First, it was realized that when the individual pursues his self-interest, he often finds that monopoly, not competition, maximizes profit. Untrammelled freedom to compete becomes a license to plunder and exploit. Excessive inequalities in income, wealth, and power soon develop. And so, in Econsciousness II we had Stage II-A in the late 19th and early 20th centuries marked by the Sherman and Clayton anti-trust acts and the adoption in 1913 of the individual income and inheritance taxes designed not just to raise revenue but to reduce inequality.

In the depression of the 1930's, we entered Stage II-B when we recognized that society, acting through government, has to take increasing responsibility for the jobless and the aged. Unemployment compensation, old age insurance, and the first public works programs resulted.

Third, in the post-World-War-II period, we entered Stage II-C. We became increasingly aware of the problem of externalities, especially the pollution costs that are inflicted on third parties instead of being absorbed by producers and consumers. And government at last took seriously its role in ending poverty and economic discrimination.

I group these three developments together as a subset of Econsciousness II because they represent a single stage in individual morality. All through stage

II the individual entrepreneur, the individual profit and income seeker, is still pursuing his own interest. He relegates to government the job of overcoming social problems that are created in that pursuit. In effect, he lets the government take care of his economic conscience. He pays the piper in the form of higher taxes and submission to regulatory restrictions. But within that framework, the pursuit of private profit and private interest is still his guiding light. It is on that assumption that most public policies dealing with private business activity have to be formulated.

But is there also an emerging Econsciousness III in which the private producer is beginning to let the public interest play a significant role in business decisions? Perhaps a new perception of self-interest is developing: Unless concern for the poor and the black, for environmental quality, for urban revival is built into business decisions, disenchantment with big business may turn into punitive legislation or revolt.

Milton Friedman insists that spending corporate money for such social purposes is a simple case of cheating the stockholders. The business of business is business, and nothing else. Many business managers and owners agree with Friedman and remain firmly planted in Econsciousness II with an Allah-be-praised reverence for profits. Some, indeed, still belong to the shrinking group of public-be-damned Neanderthals who remain mired in Econsciousness I.

But a growing number are showing some visible signs of greening. Perhaps, for some, it is a matter of image—they don't like being singled out as, say, environmental cop-outs, stinkers, and swillers. For them, it is not an exercise in altruism, not a change in individual morality, but a response to changing public morality, a recognition that they can clean up their image only by cleaning up the public's air and water.

That leaves, finally, a small but growing number of business leaders who are boldly plugging the social interest into their private decisions, even when this means some diminution of profits. Altruism sweeping the country's board rooms? Hardly. But enough of a new awareness and responsiveness to the public interest to suggest that the yeast of change is working in the right direction, perhaps even giving substance to a nascent Econsciousness III.

Clearly, without some redirection of economic activity—chiefly, by collective action, but aided by private initiative—economic growth will not become synonymous with social advance and human fulfilment, with a rising quality of life and falling inequality of income and power. That will require changes in our focus, in our priorities, and in our outer-directed involvement. As the late Whitney Young often reminded us, in his favorite quote from ancient Greece, "there will be peace and justice in Athens at last when those who are *not* injured are as indignant as those who *are*."

[1] To sharpen the issue, I will occasionally couch the argument in terms of the contrasting views and approaches of ecologists and economists. I use the term "ecologist" not in the technical sense of a natural-systems biologist, but as a proxy of "non-economist environmentalists," for the new breed of social critic whose deepest concern is the rape of the environment.

[2] Robert J. Lampman, Testimony before the Senate Sub-

committee on Employment, Manpower, and Poverty, March 23, 1971.

[3] See Chapter 13 of Charles L. Schultze et al, *Setting National Priorities: The 1973 Budget,* Washington, Brookings, 1972. In current dollars (i.e., allowing for inflation), Schultze and his colleagues foresee a rise of $1047 billion in 1971 to $1690 billion in 1977, a rise of $643 billion. Even with the resulting automatic growth of federal revenues from a full-employment-equivalent level of some $245 billion in fiscal 1973 to $340 billion in fiscal 1977, the "built-in" growth of federal expenditures would absorb virtually all of this $95 billion rise in revenues, leaving only $5 billion as a net fiscal dividend for financing program expansion *(Ibid,* pp. 412–419).

[4] *Ibid,* p. 375

[5] In the Godkin Lectures, in 1966, I put this point as follows: "If, as *by-products* in our quest for growth, we destroy the purity of our air and water, generate ugliness and social disorder, displace workers and their skills, gobble up our natural resources, and chew up the amenities in and around our cities, the repair of that damage should have first call on the proceeds of growth. If the damage is essentially a private cost forced on society, as in the case of industrial effluents and smoke discharge, it should be forced back on those private units. But much of the problem and the cost can be met only by government. (If we could isolate that part of it which is a direct cost or byproduct of growth . . . we should probably make a subtraction each year from our total output, an adjustment of our GNP figures, to take account of it.") Heller, *New Dimensions of Political Economy* (Cambridge: Harvard University Press, 1966), p. 111.

[6] Robert J. Lampman, "Recent U.S. Economic Growth and the Gain in Human Welfare," pp. 143–162 in Walter W. Heller (ed.), *Perspectives on Economic Growth* (New York: Random House, 1968).

Daniel J. Boorstin

Technology And Democracy

Daniel J. Boorstin

Technology and Democracy

TONIGHT I HAVE TAKEN FOR MY TITLE "Technology and Democracy," and I want to share with you some of the explorations and hypotheses and hunches that I have been developing in relation to the third volume of *The Americans*. The volume will be called *The Democratic Experience*. In that work as a whole I have been trying to discover what is distinctive about American life, what has characterized American civilization. Tonight I am going to talk about one aspect of that exploration which grows out of the effort to discover what we mean by democracy.

One of the most interesting and characteristic features of democracy is, of course, the difficulty of defining it. And this difficulty has been compounded in the United States where we have been giving new meanings to almost everything. It is, therefore, especially easy for anyone to say that democracy in America has failed. Tonight I would like to make a contrary suggestion drawn from a tentative definition. Democracy as it is used by political scientists usually describes a form of government by the people, either directly or through their elected representatives, but I would suggest that a democratic society is one which is governed by a spirit of equality and dominated by the desire to equalize, to give everything to everybody. This in the later 20th century has had certain consequences, and tonight I would like to explore some of these consequences which may give us some clues to the fulfillment and the meaning and the hopes of democracy.

The characteristic wealth and skills and know-how and optimism of our country have dominated this quest. I would like to talk about how the use of technology to democratize our experience has given our experience and our hopes a quite new shape. This evening I will be talking then about the consequences of democracy, not for government but for experience. And my first and overshadowing proposition is that our problems arise not from our failures but from our successes. Of course no success is complete; only death is final. But I suggest that we have come closer to attaining our professed objectives than any other society of comparable size and extent, and I also suggest that it is from this that our problems arise. What are the consequences for your experience and for mine of the effort to democratize life in America? And especially the consequences of our fantastic success in industry and technology and in invention?

I

I will mention four of these consequences and begin

with what I call *attenuation,* a word which means the thinning-out, the thinning-out or the flattening of experience. We might call this the democratizing of experience. It might otherwise be described as the decline of poignancy. One of the consequences of our success in technology, of our wealth, of our energy and our imagination, has been the removal of distinctions, not just between people but between everything and everything else, between every place and every other place, between every time and every other time. For example, television removes the distinction between being here and being there so that we are often more there when we are here than when we are there. And the same kind of process, of thinning-out, of removing distinctions, has appeared in one area after another of our lives.

For example, in the seasons. One of the great unheralded achievements of American civilization was the rise of transportation and refrigeration, the development of techniques of canning and preserving meat, vegetables, and fruits in such a way that it became possible to enjoy strawberries in winter, to enjoy fresh meat at seasons when the meat was not slaughtered, to thin out the difference between the diet of winter and the diet of summer. There are many unsung heroic stories in this effort.

One of them, for example, was the success of Gustavus Swift in Chicago, his success in building refrigerator cars. In order to make fresh meat available at a relatively low price to people all over the country, it was necessary to be able to transport it from the West, where the cattle were raised, to the Eastern markets and the cities where population was concentrated.

Gustavus Swift found the railroad companies unwilling to manufacture refrigerator cars. They were afraid that, if refrigeration were developed, the cattle would be butchered in the West and then transported in a more concentrated form than when the cattle had to be carried live. The obvious consequence, they believed, would be to reduce the amount of freight. So they refused to develop the refrigerator car. Gustavus Swift went ahead and developed the refrigerator car only to find that he had more cars than he had use for. The price of fresh meat went down in the Eastern cities, and Gustavus Swift had refrigerator cars on his hands. He then sent agents around the country, to the South and other parts of the country, and tried to encourage people to raise produce which had to be carried in refrigerator cars. One of the consequences of this was the development of certain strains of fruit and vegetables, especially of fruit, which would travel well. The development, for example, of the peaches for which Georgia has become famous was in part a result of his effort to encourage people to raise something that he could carry in his refrigerator cars.

There were other elements in this story which we can easily forget, but we can discover some of the subtlety of it if we begin to think about how central heating and air conditioning have affected our attitude toward the seasons, toward one time and another. Nowadays visitors from abroad note that, wherever you are in our country, it is not unusual to find that in winter it is often too warm indoors and in summer, often too cool.

But the development of central heating had other

less obvious consequences. For example, as people built high-rise apartments in the cities they found it impossible to have a fireplace in every room. You could not construct a high building with hundreds of apartments and have enough room for the chimneys. So central heating was developed and this became a characteristic of city life. As central heating was developed, of course it was necessary to have a place to put the machinery, and the machinery went in the cellar. But formerly people, even in the cities, had used their cellars to store fruit and vegetables over the winter. When you heated up the basement, of course it was no longer possible to store potatoes or other vegetables or fruit there. This increased the market for people who were carrying fresh fruits and vegetables by refrigerator cars and from truck farms outside the cities, and this had the result of accelerating the tendency toward equalizing the seasons and equalizing the diet of people all over the country.

Also important in attenuating experience was the development of what I would call homogenized space, especially the development of vertical space as a place to live in. There is a great deal less difference between living on the 35th floor and living on the 40th floor of an apartment building than there is between living in a house in the middle of a block and living on the corner. The view is much more the same as you go up in the air. Vertical space is much more homogenized and as we live in vertical space more and more, we live in places where 'where we are' makes much less difference than it used to.

An important element in this which has been a product of American technology is, of course, glass. We forget that the development of the production of glass in a way which made it possible to have large plates that you could look through was an achievement largely of American technology in the 19th century. Of course, one by-product was the development of the technology of bottling, which is related to some of the levelings out of seasons which I have mentioned before in relation to food. But we forget that, when we admire those old leaded glass windows which we see in medieval or early modern buildings, what we are admiring is the inability of people to produce plate glass. The reason why you had to have the little pieces leaded was that it was impossible to make a large plate. When a large plate of glass became technologically possible, this affected daily life in the United States. It affected merchandising, for example, because the "show window" became possible in which you could, with a relatively unobstructed view, show garments and other large objects in a way to make them appealing to people who passed by. But glass was also important in producing one of the main characteristics of modern American architecture—an architecture in which there is relatively less difference between the indoors and the outdoors than elsewhere. And that is one of the great functions of glass in modern architecture.

While we have the attenuation of places and times, we also have the attenuation of occasions and events. One of the more neglected aspects of modern technology is what I would call the rise of repeatable experience. It used to be thought that one of the characteristics of life, one of the things that distinguished being alive from being dead was the uniqueness of the individual moment. Something happened which could never happen again. If you missed it then you were out of luck. But the growth of popular photography, which we can trace from about 1881 when Kodak #1 went on the market, was really the first step in the success of providing repeatable experience. If you had seen this baby when he was so cute, you could still see him that way right now if you were so unlucky as to be in the living room with the parents who wanted to show you. Kodak #1 was a great achievement and was the beginning of our taking for granted that there was such a thing as a repeatable experience.

The phonograph, of course, began to become workable in about 1877. You can see some of the earliest examples if you come to The National Museum of History and Technology which I direct in Washington. We have there the original Edison machine and the Berliner machine and others. The rise of the phonograph was, of course, the creation of the opportunity to repeat an audible experience. Now if you want to hear the voice of Franklin Delano Roosevelt, you can hear his voice. It is not difficult at all, as you can simply listen to the phonograph records. At the recent opening of our Woodrow Wilson Center for International Scholars at the Smithsonian Institution, part of the dedicating ceremony was the playing of a record with the voice of Woodrow Wilson. It was not a very warm voice, but it was identifiable as a distinctive voice. The growth of the phonograph, then, has accustomed us to the fact that experience is not a one-time thing. It can be repeated.

When we watch the Winter Olympics in our living-rooms and see the ski jumper in the 70-meter jump who makes a mistake or who performs very well, we can see the same performance just a minute later with all the failures and successes pointed out. Is instant replay the last stage in the technology of repeatable experience?

In the attenuating of events there is another element (which I have described in a little book called *The Image*). It is what I call the "pseudo-event." As more and more of the events which have public notice are planned in advance, as the accounts of them are made available before they happen, then it becomes the responsibility of the event to live up to its reputation. As that happens, the spontaneity of experience, the unpredictableness of experience, dissolves and disappears. The difference between the present and the future becomes less and less. Another aspect of this, of course, is the rise of insurance, for insurance is a way of reducing the difference between the future and the present. You reduce risks by assuring yourself that, if your house burns down, at least you will have the money so you can rebuild it. In this sense, insurance, especially casualty insurance, provides a way of thinning out the difference between present and future, removing the suspense and the risk of experience.

I would like to speak for a moment about property, and some of the consequences of the democratizing of property. You will recall that John Locke (in his classic defense of property in his *Essay on Civil Government*) argued that because property is the product of the mixing of a person's labor with an object, no government has the right to take it without his consent. This simplistic conception of property has dominated a great deal of political and economic thinking. In fact, it was very prominent in the thinking of the authors of the Declaration of Independence and of the Founding Fathers of the Constitution. It was based on a state of life in which there was something very poignant and characteristic about owning something. If you owned it, you had the right to exclude people from it. You had the pleasures of possession.

But what has happened to property in our society? Of course the most important new form of property in modern American life is corporate property: shares of stock in a corporation. And the diffusion of the ownership of shares, which is a fact that people are not sufficiently aware of but which is one of the most prominent features of American life, has been extremely important. There are companies, of course, like AT&T which have as many as a million stockholders. What does it mean to be a stockholder? You are a lucky person. You own property and you have some shares. So what? One doesn't need to be rich or even middle class in this country to own shares of stock. But very few of my friends who own shares of stock know precisely what it means or what are their legal powers as a stockholder. They are solicited to send in their proxies—by somebody who has a special interest in getting them to vote for something or other. They feel very little pleasure of control; they don't have the sense of wreaking themselves on any object. Yet this—a share of stock—is the characteristic and most important form of property in modern times. This property, too, is attenuated.

Other developments in American life concerning property have had a similar effect. For example, the development of installment and credit buying. This phenomenon first grew in connection with the wide marketing of the sewing machine and then developed in relation to the cash register, but its efflorescence has come with the automobile. When it became necessary to sell millions of automobiles—and necessary in order to keep the machinery of our society going to sell automobiles to people who could not afford to lay out the cost of an automobile—it was necessary to find ways of financing their purchases. Installment and credit buying were developed. One of the results is that people became increasingly puzzled over whether they did or did not (and if so in what sense) own their automobile. Of course, it is not uncommon for people to divest themselves of their physical control of an object like an automobile or a color television set before they have really acquired full ownership—and then to enter on another ambiguous venture of part ownership.

Another aspect of this is the rise of franchising: the development of what I would call the semi-independent businessman. In the United States today between 35 percent and 50 percent of all the retail merchandising is done through franchised outlets. Well, of course, we all know what a franchised outlet is; a typical example would be a McDonald's Hamburger stand or an outlet in which the person who is in control of the shop has been authorized to use a nationally advertised name like Midas Mufflers or Colonel Sanders' Kentucky Fried Chicken. He is then instructed in the conduct of his business. He must meet certain standards in order to be allowed to continue to advertise as a Holiday Inn or Howard Johnson or whatever. And he is in business "for himself." Now what does that mean? If you go into a franchised outlet and you find the hamburger unsatisfactory, what would you do? Whom would you complain to? The man who runs the shop has received his instructions and his materials from the people who have franchised him. It is not his fault. And, of course, it's not the fault of the people at the center who franchised him because the shop is probably badly run by the franchisee. This phenomenon grew out of the needs of the automobile because in order to sell Fords or any other automobiles, it was necessary to have an outlet which would take continuous responsibility for stocking parts. Then the purchaser could replace that part at the place where he had purchased the car. After automobile franchising came the franchising of filling stations. People wanted some assurance about the quality of the fuel they put in their cars; they were given this by the identification of what they purchased with some nationally adver-tised brand in which they had confidence.

Now perhaps the most important example of attenua-tion, of the decline of poignancy in our experience in relation to property, is so obvious and so universal that it has hardly been discussed. That is packaging. Until relatively recently if you went into a store to buy coffee, you would have to bring a container to the grocery store, and the grocer would ladle out the coffee to you. Packaging however, began to develop in this country after the Civil War. In a sense it was a by-product of the Civil War because the necessities of the War (especially the need to package flour) pro-duced certain innovations which were important. And later there were decisive, although what seem to us rather trivial, innovations. For example, the invention of the folding box was important. Until there was a way to make boxes which could be transported and stored compactly, it was impossible or impractical to use them for industrial purposes. The folding box and certain improvements in the paper bag, such as the paper bag that had a square bottom so that it could stand up and on the side of which you could print an advertisement—these were American inventions.

If we will risk seeming pompous or pedantic, we can say that the most important consequences of packaging have been epistemological. They have had to do with the nature of knowledge and they have especially had the effect of confusing us about what knowledge is, and what's real, about what's form and what's substance. When you think about a Winston cigarette, you don't think about the tobacco inside the cigarette; you never see that. You think about the package. And in one area after another of American life, the form and the content become confused, and the form becomes that which dominates our consciousness. One area perhaps in which this has ceased to be true, happily or otherwise, is the area which I have always thought of as an aspect of packaging; namely, clothing. In the United States, we have developed ready-made clothing in such a way as to obscure the differences of social class. Somehow or other these differences seem to become more and more minimal nowadays!

All around us we see attenuation—as our technology has succeeded, as we have tried to make everything available to everybody. The very techniques we use in preparing our food, in transporting our food, in controlling the climate and temperature of the rooms we live in, the shapes of the buildings in which we do business and reside, the ways we look at past experience—in all these ways our experience becomes attenuated. As we democratize experience, the poignancy of the moment, of the season, of the control of the object, of the spontaneous event declines.

II

Now to a second consequence of the success of our technology for our daily experience. This is what I would call the *decline of congregation*. Or it might be called a new segregation. This is the consequence of increasingly organized and centralized sources of anything and everything. Example: Rebecca at the well. Last fall I published an article in the issue of *Life* magazine which was intended to celebrate the 25th anniversary of the introduction of television into this country. I entitled the article at first "Rebecca at the TV set," but my friends at *Life* said, "Rebecca who?" Deferring to their greater, wider knowledge of American life and of the literariness of the American people, instead we called it simply "The New Segregation." But when Rebecca lived in her village and needed to get water for the household, she went to the well. At the well she met the other women of the village; she heard the gossip; she met her fiancé there, as a matter of fact. And then what happened? With the progress of democracy and technology, running water was introduced; and Rebecca stayed in the kitchenette of her eighth floor apartment. She turned the faucet on and got the water out of the faucet; she didn't have to go to the well anymore. She no longer had the opportunity to collect the gossip and she would have to find other ways to meet her fiancé. This is a parable of the problem of centralizing sources of everything.

Another example which we forget is in the case, not only of running water, but of sanitary services. The growth of centralized plumbing was itself, of course, a necessary by-product of the development of the skyscraper and the concentration of population in high buildings. You had to have effective sanitary facilities. But we forget other features of this development. Even those of us who have never made much use of the old "privy" know that the privy characteristically had more than one hole in it. Why was this? This is not peculiar simply to the privy. It's also the case with the sanitary facilities in many older buildings, even in the medieval buildings where we know of these in Europe. The development of centralized plumbing led to privatizing; the privy was the wrong word for the old facility. The privatizing of the bodily functions made them less sociable. People engaged in them in private.

The most dramatic example today of the privatizing of experience by centralizing a facility is, of course, television. We could start with the newspaper for that matter. The town crier communicated the news to people in their presence. If you wanted to hear it you had to be there or talk to somebody else who was there when he brought the news. But as the newspaper developed, with inexpensive printing, the messages were brought to you and you could look at them privately as you sat by yourself at breakfast. Television

is perhaps one of the most extreme and dramatic examples of the decline of congregation. Until the development of television, if you wanted to see a play
you had to go out to a theater; if you wanted to hear
a concert, you had to go to a concert hall. These perfor-
mances were relatively rare. They were special events.
But with the coming of television, everybody acquired
his private theater. Rebecca had her theater in her
kitchen. She no longer needed to go out for entertainment.

The centralized source, the centralizing of the source
then led to the isolating of the consumer. Now, of
course, much was gained by this; but one of the prices
paid was what I call the decline of congregation. Congregation being the drawing together of people—as
we are drawn together here tonight in the physical
presence of one another—where we can enjoy and
react to and respond to the reactions and feelings of
our fellows.

III

Now there is a third consequence of our technological success in democratic America which I would call
the new determinism or *the rising sense of momentum*.
Technology has had a deep and pervasive effect on
our attitude toward history and especially on the
citizen's attitude toward his control over the future.
In the 17th century, of course, the Puritans spoke about
Providence; that was a characteristic way of describing
the kind of control that God exercised over futurity.

In the 19th century when people became more scientifically minded, they still retained some notion of foresight in the form of the concept of destiny or mission or purpose. But in our time in this country we have developed a different kind of approach toward futurity; and this is what I would call the concept of momentum. Momentum in physics is the product of a body's mass and of its linear velocity. Increasing scale and speed of operation increase the momentum. One of the characteristics of our technology and especially of our most spectacular successes has been to increase this sense of momentum. I will mention three examples, all of which are obvious; examples in which the development came as a result of international pressure, and which produced a phenomenon of great mass and velocity and then which became very difficult to stop.

The first example is, of course, atomic research. The large-scale concerted efforts in this country to build an atomic bomb began and were accelerated at the time of World War II because of rumors that the Nazis were about to succeed in the first nuclear fission. When this information became available, national resources were massed and organized in an unprecedented fashion; futurity was scheduled and groups were set to work in all parts of the continent exploring different possible ways of finding the right form of uranium or of some other element. And the search for the first atomic chain reaction, which was accomplished at my University of Chicago, went on.

One of the more touching human aspects of this story is the account, now well chronicled by several historians, of the frantic efforts of the atomic scientists,

the people who had been most instrumental in getting
this process started (Albert Einstein, Leo Szilard, and
James Franck among others) when they saw that the
atomic bomb was about to become possible, to persuade the President of the United States either not
to use the bomb or to use it only in a demonstration
in mid-Pacific. Such a use, they urged, would so
impress the enemy with the horrors of the bomb that
the enemy would surrender without any need to use
the bomb against a live target. They pursued this purpose with a desperation that even exceeded the energy
that they had shown in developing the bomb; but,
of course, they had no success. They could develop
the bomb, but they couldn't stop it. Why? There were
many reasons, including President Truman's reasonable belief that use of the bomb could save hundreds
of thousands of lives and shorten the War. But surely
one reason was that there had already been too much
investment in the bomb. Billions of dollars had gone
into the making of it. People were organized all over
the country in various ways. It was impossible to stop.

Another example of this kind of momentum is the
phenomenon of space exploration. I happen to be an
enthusiast for space exploration so that the fact that
I describe this momentum doesn't mean that I think
it necessarily a bad thing. Nevertheless as a historian,
I am increasingly impressed by the phenomenon of
momentum in our time. Billions of dollars were spent
in developing the machinery for going off to the moon
or going then to Mars or elsewhere. The mass of the
operation is enormous. The velocity of it is enormous,
and it becomes virtually impossible to stop. The recent
problem with the SST is a very good example of course.

The consequences of unemployment, of dislocation in the economy, are such that it becomes every year more difficult to cease doing what we are already doing.

A third example, more in the area of institutions, is foreign aid: the international pressures to give foreign aid to one country or another. You have an enormous mass of wealth being invested, a great velocity with lots of people going off all over the world and performing this operation, giving aid, and it becomes almost impossible to stop it. Then people resent the decline of aid and consider it a hostile act even though they might not have felt that way if you hadn't started the aid in the first place. Foreign aid is, I think, the most characteristic innovation in foreign policy in this century.

Each of these three enterprises illustrates the attitude of the American citizen in the later 20th century toward his control over experience. Increasingly the citizen comes to feel that events are moving, and moving so fast with such velocity and in such mass that he has very little control. The sense of momentum itself becomes possible only because of our success in achieving these large purposes which no other democratic society, no other society before us, had even imagined.

IV

Now what does this bring us to? Before I come to my fourth and concluding point on the ways in which the successes of democracy have affected our experience, I would like briefly to recall some of the remedies that have been suggested for the ills of democracy and the problems of democracy in the past. Al Smith once said, "All the ills of democracy can be cured with some more democracy." I must confess, though I admire Al Smith for some of his enterprises, the Empire State Building for example, I don't admire his wisdom in many other ways, and I think he was on the wrong track here. In fact, I would say that I might sum up the democratic paradoxes that I have been describing in the slogan which I might have used as the title of my lecture tonight if you wouldn't have thought it flip, and that is, "Getting there is *all* the fun." Is there a law of democratic impoverishment? Is it possible that democratizing enriches experience but democracy dilutes experience?

Example: photography. Before the invention of photography, it was a remarkable experience to see an exact likeness of the Sphinx or of Notre Dame or of some exotic animal or to see a portrait of an ancestor. Then as photography was publicized in the beginning of the 1880's and coming down to this century, it opened up a fantastic new range of experience to people. Suddenly they were able to see things they had never been able to see before. And then what happened? Everybody had a camera, or two or three cameras; and everywhere he went he took pictures and he came home and then he had to find a victim, somebody to show the pictures to. And this became more and more difficult. While photography was being introduced, while this new technique was being introduced, it was life-enriching and vista-opening; but once it was achieved, once everybody had a camera, the people were looking in their cameras instead of looking at the experience. It had an attenuating effect; the result was that a picture came to mean less and less, simply because people saw pictures everywhere.

Another example is, of course, the phonograph. Has the phonograph—in its universal later 20th century uses—necessarily made people more appreciative of music? In the 1920's when I was raised in Tulsa, Oklahoma, I had never heard an opera, nor had I really heard any classical music properly performed by an orchestra. But in our living room we had a wind-up Victrola, and I heard Galli Curci singing arias from Rigoletto, and I heard Caruso, and I heard some symphonies, and it was fantastic. And then HiFi came and everybody had a phonograph, a HiFi machine or a little transistor radio which you could carry with you and hear music anytime.

Now I walk into the elevator in an office building, and I hear Beethoven. Sitting in the airplane coming here, I heard Mozart coming out of the public address system. Wherever we go we hear music whether we want to hear it or not, whether we are in the mood for it or not. It becomes an everywhere, all-the-time thing. The experience is attenuated. And I suggest that one of the most serious consequences of all this is the attenuation of community itself. What holds people together? What has held people together in the past? For the most part, it has been their sense of humanity, their pleasure in the presence of one another and feeling for another person's expression, the sound of his voice, the look on his or her face. But the kind of community I describe increasingly becomes attenuated. People are enjoying the community all by themselves.

This leads then to certain desperate quests in American life. These, the by-products of our success, are clues to the vitality and energy of our country, to the quest for novelty to keep life interesting and vistas open, to the quest for community and the quest for autonomy. Can we innoculate ourselves against these perils of our technological success? Samuel Butler once said, "If I die prematurely, at any rate I shall be saved from being bored by my own success." And our problem, I think, is partly that.

And now a fourth characteristic of the relation of technology to democracy in our time: *the belief in solutions.* One of the most dangerous popular fallacies—nourished by American history and by some of our most eloquent and voluble patriots—is the notion that democracy is attainable. There is a subtle difference between American democratic society and many earlier societies in respect to the extent to which their ideals could be attained. The objectives of other societies have for the most part been definable and attainable. Aristocracy and monarchy present ideals for a society which are attainable. Even totalitarianism presents objectives which can be attained in the sense in which the objectives of democracy never can be.

This nation has been a place of renewal, of new beginnings for nations and, in a sense, for man. Vagueness has been a national resource. The vagueness of the continent, the mystery of our resources, the vagueness of our social classes, the misty miasma of our hopes. Our society has been most distinctively a way of reaching rather than of finding. American democracy properly speaking has been a process and not a product, a quest and not a discovery. But a great danger which has been nourished by our success in technology has been the belief in solutions. For technological problems there *are* solutions. It is possible to set yourself the task of developing an economic and workable internal combustion engine, a prefabricated house, or a way of reaching the moon. Technological problems are capable of solutions.

We are inclined then, using the technological problem as our prototype, to believe that somehow democracy itself is a solution, a dissolving of the human condition. But we should have learned, and even the history of technology—especially the history of technology in our democratic society—should have taught us otherwise. In human history in the long run there are no solutions but only problems. Henry Ford once heard the objections of a friend as Ford was talking about his hopes for giving everybody an automobile, and the friend said, "You know, if you get these automobiles on the road, it's going to create problems. It's going to scare all the horses. There'll be lots of accidents and it won't be good at all." And Henry Ford is reputed to have said, "There will be no problem because there will no longer be any horses on the road. Everybody will have an automobile, and that will be the end of our problem." Now of course, in a sense Ford was right; but more profoundly, of course, he was wrong.

Every seeming solution is a new problem. When you democratize the speedy automobile and give everybody an automobile, the result is a traffic jam; and this is the sense in which the "solution" of technological problems presents us with obstacles in

the way of the fulfillment of what is human in our
society. When we think about American democratic
society, then, we must learn not to think about a condition but about a process; not about democracy but
about the quest for democracy, which we might call
democratizing. The most distinctive feature of our system is not a system but a quest, not a neat arrangement
of men and institutions, but a flux. What other society
has ever committed itself to so tantalizing, so fulfilling,
so frustrating a community enterprise?

To prepare ourselves for this view of American
democracy there are two sides to our personal need,
and I will mention these briefly in conclusion. One
is on the side of prudence and wisdom; the other on
the side of poetry and imagination.

On the side of prudence, there is a need for a sense
of history. We must remember that we live in the
prison of history. The past boxes us in, qualifies our
hopes and our possibilities. Only by realizing the
boundaries that we have been given can we discover
how to reach beyond them. Only so can we have the
wisdom not to mistake passing fads for great movements, not to mistake the fanaticisms of a few for the
deep beliefs of the many, not to mistake fashion for
revolution. This wisdom is necessary if we are to secure sensibly the benefits of a free society for those
who have for whatever reason been deprived of its
benefits. We were not born yesterday, nor was the
nation. And between the day before yesterday and
yesterday crucial events have happened. We can discover these and come to terms with these only through
history. As Pascal said, "It is only by knowing our
condition that we can transcend it." Our technology

brings us the omnipresent present. It dulls our sense of history, and if we are not careful it can destroy it. We in the U.S.A. are always living in an age of transition. We always have. Others have flourished in the sense that they live in the climax of history. We must flourish in the sense that the climax is always in the future. By keeping that suspense alive, we can prepare ourselves for the shocks of change.

And finally, on the side of poetry and imagination, how do we keep alive the spirit of adventure, what I would call the exploring spirit? This should be the easiest because it is the most traditional of our achievements and efforts. We must remember that we live in a new world. We must keep alive the exploring spirit. We must not sacrifice the infinite promise of the unknown, of man's unfulfilled possibilities in the universe's untouched mysteries, for the cozy satisfactions of predictable, statistical benefits. Space exploration is a symbol. The other evening, I had the pleasure of talking with Thor Heyerdhal, the *Kon Tiki* man, whose most recent venture was the Ra expedition in which he explored the possibilities of men having come from Egypt or elsewhere in the Mediterranean to this continent long ago in boats made of reeds. And as I talked to Thor Heyerdhal about the Ra expedition, I said that it must have been a terrible feeling of risk when you suddenly left the sight of land and got out into the open sea. It seemed to me that the fear and perils of the open sea would be the greatest. Thor Heyerdhal said not at all. He said the great dangers, the dangers of shoals and rocks, existed along the shore. The wonderful sense of relief, he observed, came when he went out into the open ocean where there was openness all around though also high waves and strong currents. The promise of American democracy, I suggest, depends on our ability to stay at sea, to work together in community while we all reach to the open horizon.

Philip Handler

Science and the Future of Man

Philip Handler

Science and the Future of Man

A FEW WEEKS AGO, engaged in the masochistic evening ritual of watching the news on television, I was
appalled by the sight of a group of Bihari, sympathetic
to West Pakistan, herded into a pen by the now venge-
ful Mukti Bahini. While I ingested hors d'oeuvres and
a martini, there were scrawny, large-eyed, large-
bellied children, fiercely fighting for a handful of grain,
evading discipline enforced by men with big sticks.
That scene, miraculously conveyed live by satellite
transmission, was abruptly interrupted by a commercial in which a semi-clad male sexpot, not quite out
of bed, in a room presumably appropriate to a successful young man-about-town, announced gravely that he
found no need to utilize his underarm spray deodorant
that morning.

This offensive contretemps suddenly seemed to
encapsulate the major problems of mankind. It was
followed in quick succession by scenes of human folly
in Ulster, along the Suez Canal, Cambodia, and Viet-

nam, a violent anti-bussing demonstration, a report on the comparative armamentaria of the United States and the Soviet Union, the funeral of two murdered policemen in New York City, an airview of a strip-mined area in Ohio, and a lengthy presentation of the life and loves of one Clifford Irving. It was difficult to escape the sensation of a world gone mad.

But mankind never has behaved more rationally; it is the quickening pace of events, instant communication, and our ever increasing numbers which seem to render the world so utterly insane. I am not about to embark upon a nostalgic plea for good old days that never were, nor do I bring facile prescriptions concerning racism, religious persecution, or national-ism—virulent afflictions which have degraded man in almost every place, in every time. My concern today is that peoples and governments, worldwide, engaged with these desperate immediacies, may neglect the truly important questions on which the ultimate fate of *Homo sapiens* now appears to hang. Let me explain.

For the scientific community, the dilemma of our times began when, after Hiroshima, Oppenheimer said that "For the first time, science has known sin." And we have never been the same. That pursuit of science, in and of itself, is a meaningful purpose of our civiliza-tion will be held as moot by many; regrettably, few are privileged to share the delight of the scientist in the compelling beauty of natural phenomena. Accord-ing to Sir Brian Flowers, " ... like the arts, science gives expression to the innermost yearnings of the human spirit and thereby enriches our lives. It pro-foundly changes our comprehension of the world around us and of our place in it."

Nevertheless, many retreat from what they regard as unacceptable or incomprehensible revelations of science: the hostile vastness of the cosmos revealed by modern astronomy; the growing evidence that life, as we know it, is the inevitable consequence of the chemical composition of the earth as it formed several billion years ago, with all living things—microbial, plant, and animal—deriving from some common ancestor; the probability that similar events have occurred many times elsewhere in the cosmos; the demonstration that, biologically, man is more closely related to the chimpanzee than is the horse to the donkey; the expectation that, one day, man's brain will be completely comprehensible in purely physical terms. Few are willing to apply themselves sufficiently to grasp the wondrous ingenuity of the photosynthetic apparatus, the elegance of the structure of DNA, which permits it both to duplicate itself and to orchestrate the multitudinous functions of the living cell, the drama of the plate tectonics, which explain the continual reforming of the earth's crust, the beauty of crystalline structures, which enable the microminiaturization of modern electronics. For those few, the loss is personal, quite akin to lack of appreciation for music, art, or poetry. But what of society?

The research which has yielded this penetrating new understanding of ourselves and of the universe has been made possible by very large investments from the public purse. We manage so great a scientific endeavor on the assumptions that we will gain yet more profound insights into the nature of our universe and of ourselves, that the truths to be learned and the generalizations to be established will be translatable into technologies that will improve the public health, the productivity of our agriculture, the quality of the food on our tables and of our already remarkable communication systems, relieve the appalling contrast between the quality of intraurban and transatlantic transportation, upgrade the quality of education at all levels, further secure the national defense, while, hopefully, alleviating the damage to our environment and providing a sufficient understanding of human behavior to permit the construction of more successful, wiser social action programs than those we have known—in sum, to improve the quality of life. Without those societal goals, the American people would undoubtedly continue to support scientific research but at a small fraction of the current level.

Hence, it is simply naive to suggest, as some do, that science is as apolitical as it is amoral. Once this multibillion dollar enterprise was accepted as a proper charge on the public purse, science entered the political arena. Neither society nor scientists can discern either a clear political or scientific basis whereby to establish priorities or status among scientific fields. Since the political domain reflects the attitudes and opinions of the lay public, rather than those of scientists, the public resources which can be marshalled in support of a given field of science depend less upon what scientists think about it than upon its political, economic, or moral appeal as perceived by nonscientists. Witness the voluntary outpouring of funds for research on cancer and sickle cell anemia.

To quote Caryl Haskins, " . . . it is only when science becomes deeply rooted as an element of high culture that a progressively innovative technology can be maintained over long periods, fusing eventually into the close partnership with which we are familiar today. And even when attained, that partnership can never be taken for granted. The maintenance of its health and vigor requires constant attention." And it is that attention which I seek from you. My point is simple. If changing social and cultural conditions render the enterprise of science no longer viable, our society will have sown the seeds of its own disintegration and decay, to be followed by the disappearance of a large fraction of the world's population, and a decline in the material conditions of human life. As Harvey Brooks has noted, "It is a mere detail whether this will come about first through some ecological disaster, through the decay and demoralization of the technological structure, or through a military holocaust."

For two decades, faith in the ultimate benefits of science was almost universally accepted; financial support increased annually and progress in all disciplines was unparalleled. The powerful insights into the biological and physical universes obtained in the last few decades truly ushered in a new era that will take on yet another dimension as we gather deeper understanding of the most intractable of all scientific objects—the human brain. It happened so rapidly that few of us have succeeded in contending emotionally with either the remote haziness of our lowly origins or the inevitable empty darkness of the future, with our lonely, seemingly purposeless passage through this trivial moment in astronomic time. However ecstatic our sense of scientific understanding, in the solitary hours of the night it affords small spiritual substitute for mankind's declining faith in revealed religion. Perhaps none is to be had.

But there can be no doubt that technology based on scientific understanding has made life enormously easier, more certain, more free of pain and rich in experience for those of us fortunate enough to have been born in one of the industrialized nations. Yet even in this regard, a chorus of stock taking has begun to mount. Indeed, the damning of all forms of technology is now a national pastime. Nuclear technology, offering cheap power and the isotopes which have served as our most powerful tool for the understanding of biological systems, seems instead to provoke visions of radioactive waste and harmful genetic mutations; power plants and heavy industry equate to pollution of air, rivers, and streams; fertilizers, insecticides, and pesticides developed for agricultural productivity and health protection are thought of as contaminants of food, of earth itself, as the destroyers of nontarget organisms; the marvel of personal transportation becomes the major source of air pollution; the extraordinary educational potential of television is transmuted into the idiot box of crass commercial materialism or the means of central thought control; the wonders of the new pharmacopoeia evoke visions of malformed infants or the destructive drug culture. We are warned that the almost triumphal selection of foodstuffs in every supermarket may convey possible carcinogens and mutagens; we are alarmed that microminiaturization of electronics may deprive us of privacy in a depersonalized machine culture; we are troubled that growing understanding of the human brain and of genetic mechanisms might bring tyranny; we are perplexed that in underdeveloped nations, introduction of primitive sanitary procedures and capital-intensive heavy industry has brought over-population, wholesale unemployment, and human degradation; we are challenged with the proposition that contraceptives threaten physiological damage after long-term usage while promoting licentiousness and destruction of the family and that they are even genocidal.

Every thoughtful individual deplores man's vandalous waste of the planet's limited resources, his fouling of his own nest, his failure to distinguish between novelty and progress, to say nothing of the misuse of science-based technology to support an undiminished human appetite for military ventures. These many problems, some painfully real, some exaggerated, some imagined, have arisen largely as a consequence of millions of personal decisions, taken in the market place or the election booth by free citizens. That these decisions have not always been wise, that many have been influenced by the sometimes subtle, sometimes blatant manipulations of the advertising media, that some reflect heedless, societally unregulated pursuit of competitive advantage by industry which has, in any case, always utilized the environment as a free economic good—all this I admit. Each represents failure to have generated a means whereby we might exercise collective public responsibility to examine, in advance, the societal consequences of each new technology before it is made generally available and, collectively also, to behave accordingly.

These easy, superficial analyses and charges lead some to urge that we abandon our technology, place a moratorium on future technical developments, and halt economic growth. But their case is weak. The fact that a given object, even a foodstuff, is man-made does not make it undesirable. Indeed, it may well be superior to any natural equivalent. Food organisms conform to designs appropriate to their own biological purposes; none, however "organic," were designed for our consumption. Untreated disease may be a natural state of man but it has little attraction. The American "love affair with the automobile" has generated a thousand problems—but it also eases life and enriches our experience, as do a hundred other technologies. Some may long for the placidity of bygone rural life—but in the variety of food, the contact with man the world over, the experience of far-off places, the assault of ideas, the freedom from pain, all in this country, except our rural poor, our most forgotten ones, live more fully than did most of mankind throughout history. Those who advocate turning back are largely upper middle-class whites who see pollution rather than jobs in the belching smokestacks.

What particularly troubles me is the easy concomitant damning of science, which is now held to account, by insufficiently understanding individuals, for all the abuses of unregulated technology—whereas I believe that science, the principal element of our high culture, is the indispensable base for the new technologies that remain our only hope for a future in which man, freed of ancient, earthly constraints, may pursue his unknown destiny with dignity and in freedom.

Hence, my alarm that changes in our national thinking now appear to operate against scientific research as an essential ingredient of our national life.

Ideologies which emphasize the affective aspects of human experience, rather than the cognitive and the analytical, advocate an antirationalism that appears to have seized the minds of some fraction of our brightest youth. I really know not how large a fraction. They now suggest that affection, tenderness, and love can substitute for reason and evidence in the management of human affairs. Would that they could—but I am dubious. These movements would diminish public esteem of our high culture in all forms, romanticizing the underprivileged and promoting the egalitarian, demanding immediate gratification of all wants for all people regardless of costs today or tomorrow. This retrogressive antirationalism is forwarded by some who also argue that science is irrelevant to truly human problems and dismiss it as an elitist activity—as most assuredly it is. Extremists who express disenchantment with science—which they confuse with its technological application—argue that, since new knowledge can be most readily used by those with political and economic power, such knowledge must inevitably lead to concentration of power and is thus inherently evil. Instead of credence that "the truth shall make you free," their slogan seems to be "beware of the truth for it will be used to enslave you"—an unworthy, unconstructive, conspiratorial judgment on Western democracy, at a time when the communications media have made us the most informed citizenry in history—the ultimate basis for assuring perpetuation of a functioning democracy.

Equally serious is the ever more frequent suggestion that some aspects of science should best be left *un*explored. The chronic resistance of all societies to the intrusion of new knowledge which might substantially alter widely held views has emerged in public repugnance at the thought of what has loosely been called genetic engineering. I, too, would be violently opposed to human cloning, for example, were it feasible. But what troubles me is that even some scientists urge that we not pursue any fundamental studies that might provide the understanding which, one day, might make such events possible, ignoring the fact that it might also provide clues to the nature of the malignant transformation of normal cells, or to the basis for autoimmune diseases. They are allied in spirit with those who condemn as racist all attempts to achieve better understanding of those data which indicate that according to current IQ testing procedures the distribution of IQs among blacks averages about 7 IQ points below those of whites, while confusing possible ill-advised social application of such information with the need to establish the validity and true meaning of the data themselves.

Book burning was ever evil; I hold resistance to the advance of scientific understanding to be its modern equivalent. Any deliberate decision *not to know* not only forecloses society's options, but it must also erode the moral fiber of the precious, fragile veneer which is civilization. And in any case, such decisions are futile—someone will learn, somewhere, sometime. Society must just as surely protect the right to undertake research by which information and understanding might be acquired as society must subsequently determine how such knowledge shall be employed. Else, we reinaugurate the Dark Ages.

Many voices decry the extent of research in medical

schools. They demand abbreviated, scientifically less rigorous medical school curricula; they insist that medical schools assume full responsibility for the health care of blocks of the population, that the faculty busy itself with grinding out the maximal number of minimally trained physicians at minimal cost for maximal public service. They foster the foolish rot that thorough education and experience in the scientific underpinning of medicine somehow dilutes or degrades the nobility of the "healing urge" of the physician. And at how tragic a price!

The character of clinical practice has dramatically altered since I joined a medical faculty. The diseases which then so dominated medical practice—bacterial infections, nutritional deficiencies, and endocrinopathies—now represent a dwindling fraction of the total clinical enterprise, thanks to research which provided the understanding necessary to successful prevention or therapy. Indeed, the overwhelming bulk of the truly useful armamentarium of today's physician has been established during my professional lifetime! Instead of those diseases, now under control at relatively small cost, current practice is dominated by the use of "half-way medical technologies," palliative, corrective measures for those disorders for which research has yet to provide sufficient understanding to permit definitive prevention or therapy. It is these exercises which so completely engage our already huge resources of hospitals and clinic facilities, physicians, nurses, technicians, etc., and cost the American public $80 billion in the present year. If this picture, so much better than in the past, so much less than we can justifiably hope for, is to be improved, if the list of diseases under control is to be extended, there is no alternative to a vigorous program of biological and clinical research. And no place better for its conduct than the medical school. Should we relax in this effort, then, the nation's health needs can never be better served than the best available to anyone today, and we must envision a United States in the year 2000 with more than twice as many doctors, nurses, technicians, hospitals, clinics, sanitoria, nursing homes, etc.—and twice as much suffering and disability. I cannot find that an attractive future, even if all of that population does have easy access to the health care delivery system, the principal demand of many well-intentioned individuals today.

The most frequently voiced causes for rejection of other forms of science-based technology are superficial and transient: exhausts from automobiles or smokestacks, beer cans on the highways, cyclamates in foodstuffs, or DDT usage in agriculture. Patently, all warrant and will receive attention. Each is amenable to a technical solution at reasonable cost and with available or obtainable scientific information. But the real problems are much more profound.

Science-based technology has been the greatest single blessing of man—but it brings with it terrible problems. Although there were warnings, these problems seem to have burst upon us sooner than we expected. As foretold by Mr. Chaplin in "Modern Times," there is great need to contemplate how human beings in industrial societies will use themselves in the near future. As our labor force increasingly engages in services rather than the production of goods, the work ethic seems to be losing its force. Job satisfaction declines, and with it productivity. We do increase our per capita productivity, but by injection of captial, thereby presumably increasing the demand for education and yet, apparently, decreasing the personal satisfaction in work itself. The ultimate consequences of this trend to the structure of our society are not predictable, but they threaten ever growing problems of personal dissatisfaction, of massive unemployment, of urban concentration and with it urban blight, violence, delinquency, illegitimacy, etc. Man, a working animal, having been liberated by his own ingenuity, may now not know what to do with himself. These problems are not amenable to repair by self-generated market forces; to face them will require wisdom and courage rare in individuals, more rare in governments.

For the first time we are confronted with the horrendous problem of hordes of marginal humans. Overseas they are displaced from the land by successive generations of ever smaller subdivision of land ownership, at home by increasingly efficient agriculture. Yet there are few opportunities in the city, and we find ourselves confronted with the need to devise an ethical penal code to deal with youthful criminals programmed by two decades in the ghetto to engage in the deviant behavior in which they are apprehended. In view of our deep concern when 6% of our labor force is unemployed, what can maintain the stability of a society in which one-third are unemployed, as in Bangladesh?

A perceptive analysis of these problems appeared in a recent issue of the British journal, "The Ecologist," in a statement entitled "A Blueprint for Survival," signed by about thirty scientists representing a variety of disciplines. The principal thrust of their message must be familiar by now: infinite growth is not possible on a finite planet with finite resources. Subsidiary thoughts include: Life itself, particularly organized human society, is exquisitely dependent upon the stability of ecosystems which become more vulnerable as they are simplified. Resource and energy use, pollution, and population will continue to grow exponentially without conscious intervention.

The peoples of the world are distributed bimodally: The industrialized world enjoys mean per capita incomes of about $2000 and the have-nots survive with mean incomes of about $125. Fifty-one percent of the world population have mean per capita incomes below $100, 18% between $100 and $500, only 6% between $500 and $1000; 25% know more than $1000 per year and ours is about $4000 per year. Worse still, the disparity grows. Although economic growth rates, as percentages, are larger in the developing than in the already industrialized nations because the former start from so much lower a base, the overwhelming bulk of the absolute annual increment in consumption of energy and nonrenewable resources occurs in the industrialized nations.

In contrast, populations grow more rapidly in the developing than in the developed world both as percentages and in absolute numbers. If the replacement size family is realized for the world as a whole by the end of this century—an unlikely event—the world's population will then be about 5.8 billion. But because of the resulting age distribution, it will not stop growing until near the end of the next century, when it will be about 8.2 billion. If, as seems more likely, replacement is achieved in the developed world by 2000 but in the developing world by about 2040, then the world's population will stabilize at nearly 15.5 billion about a century hence—four times the present size. Even the least of these is calamitous! The British group advocates a general strategy which entails checking, then reversing population growth, reducing the use of natural resources with maximal recycling, minimizing the utilization of fertilizer, while protecting wetlands, forests, tundra, and other as yet relatively unspoiled areas of the earth. For two main reasons they argue that an "optimal" population, world-wide, should certainly be no larger than it is today. First is the ability of available arable lands to sustain human populations. They argue that the "Green Revolution" is misleading—that while it has certainly bought time in averting wholesale famine, there are associated hazards. The high yields of the new strains of grain derive from application of about 25 times as much fertilizer as the old, and the phosphate cannot long be available. They believe that the structure of soils so used must break down and become infertile. The new strains are extraordinarily thirsty—yet in many places we witness even now the growth of tensions concerning water resources. Second, they believe that if society is to be stable, not only must population trends be dramatically reversed, but also the trend to urbanization must be reversed, with all societies decentralized into many smaller, planned communities of more rural character than those at present. Only thus, they argue, can we minimize transportation problems, reduce our worst social ills, and provide meaningful jobs for all. In effect, they pin the future of man on a less efficient agricul-

141

ture! Patently, natural resource depletion will prove at least as significant in giving direction to the future.

Much public attention has been given to recent computer simulations of the entire global economy, projections which portend apocalyptic collapse of human societies early in the next century. I hold little brief for these studies. The models are simplistic, the assumptions of questionable validity, and they have yet to be confronted with the vast amount of hard data available. They ignore the corrective play of market forces; that is, since the prices of resources rise with scarcity, use diminishes. They assume an already heavy death toll due to something called pollution—whatever that may be—and a rising death rate with further pollution. Yet these have been hard to prove and, if true, surely we will take drastic corrective measures. Moreover, these models ignore the power of innovative technology, such as new energy sources, efficient recycling, new, longer lasting materials and equipment, cheap, easy, reliable contraception, antipollution regulation and technology—all of which are almost certain, provided that we maintain the scientific endeavor. I am equally confident that continued agricultural research will yield yet better cereal strains which will not require such huge quantities of water and fertilizer and that we shall exploit other approaches to food production—aquiculture, new food species, etc.—all of which depend on future biological research.

Yet, even if the predicted date for doomsday is probably overpessimistic, even if man will prove more adaptable than assumed by these computer models of society, their basic underlying concepts must be correct. Without meticulous planning, conscious intervention, and a great deal of new scientific knowledge, the ultimate outcome *is* bleak. It matters little whether doomsday occurs in 2040 or 2080. The point is that at current exponential growth rates, if we lack the courage to effect large changes in our behavior, we can buy only a short delay.

Translation of that British manifesto into a working "plan" must surely become the most important political accomplishment of organized human society. But it cannot be constructed in global terms, since, lacking a world government, it must be managed by the behavior of individual nation states, both industrialized and developing. Let us briefly consider each.

We constitute the exaggerated prototype of the industrial society. American population growth is trivial when reckoned against our ability to feed ourselves and a great many others as well. But it is horrendous when multiplied by our exponentially growing per capita resource exploitation. Our 6% of the world's population now accounts for 33% of world consumption of copper and cobalt, 44% of coal, 63% of natural gas, 40% of molybdenum, 26% of silver and zinc, etc. And our appetite for these materials grows about 3 to 5% annually. Yet, even now aluminum, copper, gold, lead, mercury, molybdenum, silver, tin, zinc, natural gas, petroleum, and phosphate rock are forecast to be exhausted between the turn of the century and the year 2050 if current trends continue. I understand that such predictions are always pessimistic, but as our geologic knowledge becomes more reliable and comprehensive, such projections must become increasingly accurate. In any case, a decade or two can be of little consequence in such regards, except for the time we have to get ready. Although we are self-sufficient for one third of the 75 strategic minerals, we are entirely dependent on imports for one third, while for one third the situation is mixed. Hence, we cannot simply retreat into an economic "Fortress America."

There is already evident widespread concern for restoration of the environment. Relatively fewer people concern themselves with the supply of mineral resources; this concern is, however, a continuation of a historic political process. Government regulation of the utilization of petroleum and natural gas must soon rest on the proposition that these resources belong to the nation; hence, the companies which make them available are, collectively, a public utility or instrumentalities of the larger society—a view which the companies and their stockholders do not necessarily share. But one can scarcely consider current policy to be enlightened. Current oil import restrictions are fixed to assure the profits of our oil companies. Yet, I am told, although current oil production capacity exceeds demand, after about 1975 or 76 in the free world, projected demand will always exceed supply. Hence, as rapidly as possible we must move both to reduce the global rate of consumption and to conserve our domestic supply of this precious resource, not as a source of energy but for the long-term future of synthetic chemistry. In turn, this will require early replacement of petroleum by coal gassification, otherwise our civilization goes down not in flames but for lack of flame!

In time, national considerations must also be applied

more rigorously than today to many other minerals, to the timbering of forests, and to the "development," more properly termed "destruction," of wetlands. In other areas we do better. Pesticides, like drugs, must now be licensed before their manufacture and distribution. Pressures *are* being brought to bear on the major polluters, frequently by explicit legislative action, and the response is beginning. Even now, a great variety of approaches to population control receive increasing acceptance, here and abroad—a considerable turnaround in only one decade. In these limited senses, ours is becoming a planned society, a regrettable but inevitable event.

However, we are far from having agreed to move to the controlled, stable society required by that Blueprint for Survival, much less agreed to the means for getting there. And it is at that point where ecologists and economists appear to be at odds.

Environmentalists suggest that Americans already have a surfeit of worldly goods; they demand an early end to economic growth in the hope that, with pollution control and reduced accumulation of fabricated products, we may achieve equilibrium with the environment as soon as possible. But the economists note that the costs of undoing the historic damage to the environment and then maintaining it in a desired state may become 5 or even 10% of the GNP. If the GNP, or even the GNP per capita, were to remain constant, the costs of environmental protection would be offset only by an improvement in the quality of life, whose dollar value cannot be estimated and whose effect on human health, if any, can only be guessed at.

Patently, if we halt economic growth, the costs of

145

environmental quality would oblige each of us to forego whatever we might otherwise have done with our shares of that portion of the national GNP per capita. If all of us lived like the upper middle class, such a future might find easy acceptance. But we do not. The historic process of social improvement has been made possible entirely by the process of economic growth; for example, improved access to health care, education, and job opportunities to those on the bottom of the economic ladder, an improvement which still proceeds with heartwarming rapidity. In the last decade, the number of Americans below the federally-defined poverty line fell from 39 to 24 million—from 22 to 12 percent of a rising population. This improvement came from a 3 percent increase in mean productivity per year, an absolute increase in the number of jobs, shifts of the poor and the children of the poor from lower to higher income occupations, and considerable growth in government cash transfers, a euphemism for use of the tax mechanism to redistribute the wealth.

If the principle of zero economic growth were to be invoked, either further upward social mobility would cease or, having already decreased the per capita GNP by the costs of environmental protection, we would further require a far greater redistribution of the wealth by taxation than any we have yet considered, and to which we have certainly not yet agreed. Moreover, if economic and population growth were to halt, it seems likely that a national debt, safely incurred according to Keynesian economics, would then fall due, leading to serious depression. Hence, the economists seek some way to promote economic growth while still protecting the environment and regulating resource usage in acceptable degree. If, indeed, those computer models of our economy were trustworthy, we would be in a better position to determine the real limits to our economic growth. At this date, they remain unknown.

The success of the economists' approach will rest almost entirely on the ability of the scientific and technical community to find technical solutions to obviate these problems. I share the confidence of the economists but must emphasize the need for fundamental research if all this is to occur on an acceptable time scale. Critical to its success are the imperatives that we find substitutes for current materials, learn how maximally to recycle the stock of available materials, and secure the future of the energy supply. Since petroleum and natural gas will become unavailable in 30 to 60 years, coal gassification and breeder reactors will become imperative as the next source of energy on a large scale; in about a century, controlled fusion must become available if anything like our current civilization is to survive. However power is produced, it is, *ipso facto,* a source of pollution and will generate new problems, some predictable even now. These simply must be solved! Only science can do so!

None of what I have said is intended to be a prophecy of doom. But it is a plea for early, universal understanding of man's plight. Man *is* adaptable and science is his most powerful tool. It *is* possible for us to live in comfortable equilibrium with the planet which has spawned us. The question is, how long before these tremendous problems are recognized as the primary challenge to our national and international policy?

What fraction of our energies will we redirect from the urgent to the important? Or will we wait so long that we will have lost the opportunity to take corrective measures? Were this nation like the colony of social ants we have recently seen in China, it would be easy. Can it be done by a society whose cardinal tenet is the freedom, indeed the sanctity, of the individual? I do not know how long we have for analysis, planning, and research; but it may well have to be done within our lifetimes. Certainly, the lags between understanding, decision, implementation, and effect are such that there is little time to lose. The transition from today to that more planned society will be most painful. If we survive it, science can then help to assure a truly "Brave New World."

What then shall we say of the developing nations? Surely any inhibition on the economic growth of Bangladesh, for example, is unthinkable. Any suggestion from industrialized nations that the leaders of Bangladesh give over some fraction of their GNP, however tiny, to protection of the environment would only be regarded by them as madness. We and the other industrialized nations of the world, in the name of humanity and to ease our consciences, as well as for geopolitical reasons, are committed to some degree of technical and capital assistance to developing nations. At current levels, it is unlikely that this can include much environmental protection. More importantly, it takes but the simplest calculation to demonstrate how far such nations have yet to go economically. And I find it unlikely that the industrialized world will provide capital in the vast amounts necessary if truly significant gains are to be made by such peoples during this century.

But suppose we agree to do so! The real trial to our consciences will then come from contemplation of the consequences of their developmental success, were it at all feasible.

My point is that all estimates of the requirements for the development of Asiatic, African, and Latin American peoples turn out to have stupefying dimensions.

For example, a 50% increase in agricultural production, using otherwise current technology would demand annual application of 340,000 tons of pesticides in India alone, while guaranteeing depletion of all first grade ores of phosphate rock on the planet in a few decades. To provide the extra iron, lead and zinc, chrome, petroleum, gas, etc., to raise the annual per capita consumption level of all 3400 million current non-Americans to that of the average American would require approximately a ten-fold increase in present annual global production of these resources. And that, of course, would have to be doubled again as the world's population doubles in the next 30 years. Even then, we must contemplate the hellish vision of Calcutta with an expected population of 30 millions at the turn of the century, two thirds of whom may be unemployed. All of which is to say that the skin of this planet simply cannot afford successful development of the so-called developing nations without an absolute halt on population growth. And probably not then. I do not suggest that achievement of our material standard of living is an appropriate or desirable goal

149

for all the world. But even part way there is just not possible.

And there are dreadful ironies. The only way such peoples can *earn* needed developmental capital is to extract minerals from the earth and sell them to the industrialized nations. As this happens, the terms can surely be expected to stiffen, as we have already seen for Middle East oil. If the industrialized nations, hopelessly dependent on the others for many mineral resources, brake their own economic growth, they both diminish the market for those resources and forego the increase in capital which makes possible the economic growth of the poor nations. International sharing, almsgiving if you prefer, will then be demanded—and if we accede, the quality of life the world over will tend to be averaged out. We will be much poorer but the others only slightly richer. I doubt whether your children will enjoy it! In this sense, the current world population is already excessive! That fact, sooner rather than later, must become the primary, most painful of all political facts for mankind. Only concerted international agreement and wise action can then assure that there will be a future for man. And that fact returns us to the news clips with which we started—the reality of how difficult it is to believe that such international agreement can be attained and implemented in time. That problem demands a political, not a scientific, solution.

I cannot leave you without noting that current understanding of human biology and our genetic mechanisms offer both an extraordinary, powerful tool and a profound challenge. We are now bent on a seriously dysgenic course, by which we shall maintain alive for further reproduction thousands, if not millions, who might in a previous time have failed to survive. We are now aware of more than 1,000 distinct genetic disorders of man, of which we have detailed understanding of perhaps 150. Already perhaps one third of pediatric practice is either directly concerned with or complicated by genetic considerations. One begins to suspect that virtually every mutation compatible with life is actually abroad in our population. What shall we do with that information? The ethical problems deriving from our increasing capability to detect and either assure the survival of the unfit or destroy them, are enormous as we confront our sense of the sanctity of individual human life with the new concept of the sanctity of the human gene pool. I rather suspect that social pressure for zero population growth will, in time, ease those decisions, viz., our consciences will find it easier to agree to protect the gene pool in very early life. Each family will consider itself entitled to two "perfect" children rather than merely "two children" if it so chooses. Just as we shall learn to more readily accept "death with dignity" at the other end. The challenge will be to do so without relaxing our ethics with respect to the long period between.

The converse problem may be even more staggering. Man, the only species that knows that it is the product of evolution, today controls the numbers and activities of all other living forms. The environmental forces that formerly gave direction to his evolution are no longer operative; man shapes his own environment. I do not know if we are still evolving, but should we, if we can, shape our further evolution tomorrow? If so, in what direction? I doubt whether we shall indefinitely be content to sit idly by and "let nature take its course"—whatever that may mean in this context. If we are to intervene, we will require all the scientific and philosophic understanding we can acquire. I confess that I am reluctant to believe that we imperfect creatures will be the blind end of biological evolution.

Our society really has no choice. Since Prometheus stole the fire from the gods, man has been using energy to alter his own world. Our era began when Francis Bacon delineated the essence of the scientific method early in the 17th Century. Armed with Bacon's intellectual instrument and the fire of Prometheus, man has altered the world to suit himself, multiplying his numbers, fashioning the landscape, determining the fate of all other creatures on this planet. Now there can be no turning back. To reject science at this juncture is to invite the specters of pestilence, famine, and nuclear holocaust.

Peccei summarized it thus: "The responsibility of controlling technology, and through it of regulating the world ecosystem itself, now rests on man. He must now take upon himself functions in the cycle of life which formerly were reverently considered to be the prerogative of nature or providence and left to their inscrutable designs. The physical world and the biosphere are now so pervasively interfered with by man's actions that he has no other alternative but to accept the responsibility of being himself, the enlightened manager of his terrestrial kingdom." In that sense, the beast *Homo sapiens* has truly become Man. Never has he known so great a burden.

Leon Edel

Through a Revolving Door:
the Ecology of Humanism

Leon Edel

Through a Revolving Door:

the Ecology of Humanism

WE HAVE BEEN WEARING THE WORD "ecology" rather hard and in proposing to speak of *The Ecology of Humanism* I recognize that I am subjecting it to further strain. We seem to rediscover words as we buy clothes: and within a matter of days they are out at the elbows. Need I mention the word *paradigm* popular one or two seasons ago? Or *dichotomy*, before that? Will the word *relevant* soon become irrelevant? Ecology, however, happens to be the word I need, although I am willing to allow that it is a trifle shopworn. I want to suggest to you that humanism is as organic as our environment. It is not an isolated creation; it is not artificial. It is a complex of things, of inter-related things, and it can be polluted quite as horribly—even more horribly, I think—than our oxygen or our mercurized fish. For when we have polluted our minds, then we are worse off than savages. Their minds may be savage by our standards, but savagery is normal for savages; and it is unpolluted when it has its modes, tabus, rules, myths, proper to itself. I therefore do not apologize for the use of this popularized word. I speak of the "ecology" of humanism by design.

My thesis is simply this: learning, the study of human beings and human things for human needs and human uses, is being polluted like our rivers or our air. Speech can be polluted. Language can be polluted through a disrespect for the sound and poetry of meaning; it is polluted by a mangling of words, in the constant illiterate media-chatter, and by advertising which reinforces false meanings. All this constitutes a serious threat to our mental and emotional life: more serious, I am convinced, than anything that has occurred to mankind through the millenia save epidemics and natural disasters. When in the old oppressive days of history an Inquisition forbade men to think in certain ways, it succeeded often in stopping their mouths; but it did not stop them from thinking, it could not alter the patterns or modes of their thoughts. The mental pollution of which I speak is of a kind which actually changes our ways of thinking and even arrests them; more vicious still, it programs them. There exists brainwashing on a scale so extraordinary that we—many of us—rub our eyes in disbelief. And yet if we look closely we can see that it is actually happening: and so far as I know few have paid attention to it. Marshall McLuhan has told us this in very many ways, but he himself has tended to be so enchanted by the marvels of technology that he "comes through" as an admirer of the media more often than as a warning voice. The new forces of which I speak are changing, in spite of our constituted human nature, the entire mental landscape of our generation, and therefore the entire functioning of man. The question may be asked whether there will remain any way of arresting this seemingly irreversible trend, if we do not act soon to stem the systematic daily "input" of fantasy into the conscious and subliminal life of our young and even of those who are older. The media have become, in my opinion—and I want to say this as strongly and as loudly as I can—an extraordinary instance of pollution through addiction, like the taking of drugs. If tomorrow all the movies were to be closed, all the television and radio sets turned off, and all the newspapers ceased to publish, I suspect there would be in our society very speedily an epidemic of nervous breakdowns, eruptions of violence of feeling, at the least a universal irritation. The resounding emptiness of our social being would suddenly become audible; it would be brought into dramatic awareness. People would discover that they had lost a series of crutches and supports and substitutes for human living because they had surrendered human relations, the give and take of life, the observation of the external world, for their fixation on a little box; in a word they had made the turning of a knob an act of existence instead of a casual amusement.

Some will say that I exaggerate and that I turn a little hill into a mountain; that the entertainment gadgets and news gadgets we have created, thanks to the electric age, are benign and cheering. What more pleasing for the busy housewife performing her unwanted chores than to have the television going, or the radio, anything that can distract her from her work and mitigate its tedium? The answer is that she also is being distracted from the human process of having free thoughts, fancies, feelings. Instead her feelings, thoughts, fancies are being triggered, channelled, supplied, indeed diabolically designed and programmed by outside forces, I am reminded of the horror of *Fahrenheit* 451 when the walls become television screens. And beyond the rooms of the apartment or house in which we live, the media surround us, envelope us. I positively long for an elevator I can enter in which no music is playing, where I can hear its mechanism during a moment of quiet. I long to be able to walk without seeing great news headlines or a stand filled with pictures of female or male forms in erotic postures often as if they were simply exposing themselves in indecent fashion. And who hasn't quailed at some time before the music from a transistor carried aboard a bus by some specimen of our civilization who unconsciously forces himself upon the world by carrying sound with him. Or the act of smoking in a room when others do not want to breathe the smoke—and in the presence of "no smoking" signs. Our freedoms become tyrannies, as Charles Dickens remarked long ago. And we seem to have lost the sense of accommodation. I remember a student arguing that I infringed on her liberty by refusing to allow her to smoke during an examination. She needed it she said to soothe her nerves. But I insisted on the prohibition. After all, other students would have to breathe her smoke. I chose to be a tyrant. I saw no need to pamper her addiction.

What, you will ask, has this to do with the ecology of humanism? I will try to suggest this to you when I show you that the erosion of humanism occurs through our anarchic social conditioning or brainwashing by mechanical and other means which is swiftly regressing the masses to the most infantile modes of thought and behavior. In fact I believe that we have regressed to the point where I must explain first what I mean by humanism. Today one can take nothing for granted. I use humanism in its dictionary sense of "any system of thought or action which is concerned with merely human interests". I do not like the word "merely" since I consider human interests paramount. But I suppose the dictionary wants to distinguish between that which is human and that which is divine or extra-human. It is a human interest and a devotion to human interests to want to cure a disease. It is a non-human interest to cultivate germs in order to create a disease, as in bacteriological warfare. It is a human interest to know the past so that we do not repeat certain old mistakes and can discover new knowledge—yes, even new mistakes. To use four letter words may have a certain specific value and a certain emphasis at crucial moments, but to do so to the exclusion of the richer words in our vocabulary is a form of regression. It is like going back to make a fire by rubbing sticks, or using petroglyphs as a form of communication. Those who reduce our language to monosyllables are in effect rubbing sticks to make fire, or returning to petroglyphs without the creativity of the men who originally carved them in lava or rock. It was all very well for Thoreau to pretend he was playing Robinson Crusoe at Walden. He wanted to simplify his life; but he did not create his own tools, he used those of the society that he abjured. He did not invent a new plough or try to live in a cave. He used a prefabricated shanty and even plastered it. Let us beware of simplifications.

The ecology of humanism is then a vast series of interdependences: we learn one thing and it leads us to another. The organic nature of our body is one of the marvels—perhaps the greatest marvel—of creation: the inner checks and controls, the way in which our blood pressure or heart can mobilize to meet unfamiliar and seemingly unlearned situations, the ways in which our nerves and muscles seem equal to any and all kinds of sudden stresses which we never seem to have learned, and yet suddenly are mobilized in the service of our whole being. We are less inclined to marvel, so important is our physical being and physical response, at the richness of the mind, its capacity for gathering and holding information, and for the textures, if I can use so curious a word, of human temperament.

When Cicero used the word *humanitas* he employed a term which came to mean ultimately gentleness, kindness, consideration, ways of life in which we recognize that while our own comfort is important to us it depends no less on the comfort of others, and by certain mutualities we establish modes of behavior we call civilization. Later *humanitas* also came to incorporate the idea of intellectual life, of humane study. *Omni recto studio atque humanitate versari*—to be versed in all true study, and added Cicero "to be versed in humanity." When Balzac named his series of novels the *Comédie Humaine* he was thinking of them in contrast to Dante's *Divina Commedia*. I need not here rehearse the long disputes between those who dismissed the earthly order of life in favor of the Divine. It had the effect in the old days of making human life cheap. But we learned to reconcile the immediate with the problematical—we learned to value life and to value human potential, and this in spite of the continuing barbarisms of war. Nor do I need to deal with the neo-humanism among the intellectuals of our time, the protracted controversy of the 1930's, when Mr. Eliot and Professor Babbit exchanged their ideas about the secular and the religious. I believe Mr. Eliot was right in believing that the religious need not be excluded, for it too is a human creation; as has been said, some of the finest Gods have been the noblest works of man. But I hold even more significant to my thesis today the words of Buddha long ago: "Neither abstinence, nor going naked, nor shaving the head, nor a rough garment, neither offerings to priests, nor sacrifices to gods, will cleanse a man who is not free from delusions."

The freedom from delusions is not written into the freedom of our Constitution. On the contrary, we have so written the Constitution, that we provide freedom for our society to create as many delusions as possible, and for individuals and corporations to foist delusions upon us by the most curious and indeed powerful means. The delusions, for instance, that a society drowned in soapsuds is a clean society; the strange delusion that pictures tell an absolute truth even though the lens may be turned at an untruthful angle; the delusion that a newspaper harbors an ultimate knowledge of what is news when it interviews Martha

Mitchell on cosmic problems. Great are our delusions and self-deceptions; and great the power to foist them on a Republic of Ignorance.

Elementary psychology tells us that we learn by watching, imitating, listening, smelling, tasting, touching at various stages of our growth, during our earliest years. This is what our scientists of the computer refer to, I believe, as input. If the learning is properly acquired in an organized society, whether a tribe or a civilized group, a seemingly magical process occurs. Out of this input (an input of human stuff) we arrive at our personal output. Our nerve ends and muscles carry within them a great deal of memory. They know that if you bump your head against something one day, then the next day, at the mere glimpse of the object, you will automatically duck. At least that is what my reflexes have demonstrated to me. We learn very quickly, but we *un*learn with difficulty. The scientists call this "extinguishing" a response. It took me a little while to stop ducking every time I crossed the threshold of my kitchen where I once smacked myself very hard against an open cupboard door. This is true of all the forms of input. Today we learn languages with the aid of tape recorders and electronic machinery of various kinds; and we can achieve a magnificent input in this way. We teach language in the way it is learned by parrots or myhna birds. But something else occurs. Parrots rarely know the etymology of the words they imitate; and they certainly do not arrive, so far as we know, at a very clear idea of their meaning. In abandoning the teaching of the basic foundations of language, say the Latin foundations of so much of the spoken Western word, and the Anglo-

Saxon, we throw away the deeper understanding of language and its accretions of meaning which enabled us in reality to know more words than we learn, to guess and feel the meanings of words—a process which made us talking and writing beings. What I am suggesting is that behind learning and language there is a long historical chain that involves the most complicated kind of memory and association: this is what I mean by the ecology of our culture, the ecology of humanism.

The mass media at one stride achieve a gross and wholesale kind of input and when I speak of this I am often laughingly contradicted because so many feel that the media are peripheral to our daily lives. But we seem to forget that the advertisers do not laugh. They address themselves seriously to delivering their messages—and at prodigious expense. We may not teach Latin any more, and many other things the young used to learn in the world through simple observation and human contact; but they learn very quickly the little tunes that go with this brand and that; and a whole series of antics that accompany pictured messages to which they are exposed much more than to the actual world around them. Have you ever listened to a child insisting on a certain brand in the supermarket? That child has received the medium which is the message, as Mr. McLuhan might say; for the two are indeed one. And these sights and sounds have been received in such a series of simultaneities and speeds that there is no mistaking their presence. This is not to say that statistically the public buys everything that it encounters in the media. The sales element is another matter. I am not concerned with the statistics of salesmanship. I am concerned with the *internalizing* of this material.

But enough of theory. Let me rather tell you about a personal adventure—how my attention was first directed to this formidable subject. It occurred in the most usual way imaginable. It happened one day while I was going through a revolving door.

II

It was an actual door. I remember the time of the year and the place. It produced for me an unforgetable moment of pain, bewilderment, astonishment. But to tell you of this strange adventure I must retrace the events leading to it. I had occasion some years ago to enter a hospital; and to keep me amused it was suggested that a television set be placed in my room while I was recovering. I had up to this time escaped this modernity. Not wholly escaped, indeed, for how can one? But it had never become an obsessive object of attention in my life. The toy, gleaming white, antiseptic, stood at the foot of my bed. At my side was a pushbutton, which I believe is also called a "blabout." It gave me the power to make things flicker by, or pause: it could also silence. I was omnipotent. I controlled appearance and disappearance. I was a magician. But I found soon enough that my magic was limited. I could summon up scenes; I could not create them. The object brought into my room a twilight fluorescence. I was in a world beyond imaginable dreams. It was discontinuous, devoid of repose. We flashed from cigarette to jungle, from war to clowning, from morals to immorality, from indecencies to prayer, from piety to chewing gum. A curious want of real light, or real contrast, indeed of reality; it was all chiaroscuro and phantasmagoria—and synthetic feeling. The people seemed real; the sets seemed real; the voices were real—and yet it was unreality, save when I lit upon the world of sport. The baseball was real enough, but it too was somehow contained, unfree. It was a world of close-up, sometimes fascinating, but often claustrophobic.

I watched the news for a while, but I must say with mounting distaste. I did not like its instant quality, nor its fabricated scenery. Reporters chattered too much; they were too much in the picture. I had always been taught that reporters should be neither seen nor heard; they should work quietly and let news speak for itself. Here the reporter became the significant personage; he was always sticking his microphone aggressively into the faces of people and asking them to talk. Moreover most of the people were delighted to talk. It didn't matter what they said—no one seemed to care. There was no real filtering or editing. I expected some of the persons interviewed to say, "Young man, take this thing away from my face." But no one did. The medium turned individuals in the street into performers. I got bored very easily with so much stimulated exhibitionism.

And then for the first time I studied the visual reporting of the war in Viet Nam. I found it terrifying: not the war, for that was made to seem routine, but the way the TV reporters handled it on the battlefields. They shoved their perpetual microphones into the faces of the wounded on stretchers and asked them strategy questions even a general couldn't answer. The wounded, in a visible state of shock, instead of telling the reporters to get lost, tried their best to say something articulate, to answer—as if the television camera might give them a little bit more of the mortality they were in grave danger of losing. I thought of families across the nation in front of the little box, eating popcorn or TV dinners, and feeling the war was as routine as one's household life, or just another Western, a large shoot-out. The media boast they have made us aware of the war, brought it into our homes. This of course is nonsense. They have brought a few impersonal snapshots, of a painful kind, which blunt our sensitivity to what is really going on in Viet Nam. No one voluntarily wants to contemplate so much horror, however routine it is made to seem.

My rambles from station to station became a journey into the heart of consumer-land and into appalling banality. Within this constant talk and display of personality there was something that produced in me a grave disquiet: so many people in these "talk" shows were talking about themselves, their private tastes, their private habits, their divorces, their loves, their liver pills, their everyday doings, as if these irrelevancies were of the greatest importance to the world. I felt certain this creates a sense in the young that no one needs to have a private life: life is all exhibition and display, all revelation. The quiz questions and answers revealed a portentous ignorance, but it was the concept behind them that worried me: this was that education consists in remembering answers to questions, any old questions, statistics, geography, esoterica, erotica. I always believed education was not memory but learning where and how to find knowledge and developing

taste and discrimination. But I must apologize for such
belated discoveries of matters most persons now take
for granted. It was all there with the turning of a knob.

One particular evening lingers in my memory. I had
fallen asleep and awoke towards midnight. I thought
I would put myself to sleep again by turning on this
crepuscular fluorescence. I looked at a picture of sol-
diers pushing through jungle and thought I was seeing
the war in Viet Nam; then I turned to another station
and it was showing different scenes of the war. I shut-
tled between the two to discover one was a film about
jungle war, an old fiction, the other the real thing:
and I realized how easy it was to become confused
between that which purports to be news-reality and
that which is film fantasy, but seemingly quite as real.
I then came on a spectacle of Roman life—chariots,
races, angry clashes of arms, orgies, poisonings, quail-
ing Christians about to be thrown to the lions, with
the cameras looking right into the big open hungry
mouths of the lions. This was uncomfortable. I
switched to another station and it was a news story
of the opening of some show at the Colosseum in
Columbus Circle, quite different from the Roman
Colosseum. They had a model in a bathing suit display-
ing a pair of legs and thighs, and suddenly in walked
a lion—it was a very leonine evening—a great big,
lazy, tranquilized lion, the day-dream of a publicity
man with a hangover. Presently the lion yawned and
showed his sharp teeth as in the Roman film. I thought
we were to have some fanciful version of Beauty and
the Beast, only the beast in this instance, in spite of
his glazed eyes and his *ennui*, proceeded then and
there to sink his teeth into the model's thigh—some

wrong cue, some strange miscalculation. The screams and horror were more painful than anything in the Roman picture. I rang for the nurse to bring me a tranquilizer.

These were my adventures in the hospital: they were harmless enough you will say. They happen in every household all the time. After a day or two I had had enough of my plaything. I read books, did some writing, and in due course I was released from my enforced leisure. It became a remote dream—was forgotten, in the way we forget long hours of hospital boredom and pain. The details are a blur, a dead end of memory. Nurses, surgeons, audiovisual distractions, political speeches, newscasts, lions, Romans, beauties, all the gratuitous advice about soap and supermarkets slipped into a limbo of disremembrance. Forgotten? One never knows. One day, several months later I came away particularly tired from a two-hour lecture, with a great dryness in my throat. I walked out into the autumn chill, and I remember I was in a bit of a hurry to get to my office down the street. En route, I passed a sandwich and coffee shop—one of a well-known chain in New York. I had the thought that I might buy a container of coffee, to sip at my desk. Thus it was that I entered the revolving door. Out of the dark backward and abysm, as if someone had pressed an electric switch in my brain, or as if I were some kind of special memory machine, there began to sing within me, *fortissimo*—as if played by an orchestra of one hundred, or a thousand, musicians—a tune, a silly, janging, trivial tune, which assured me that a certain kind of coffee, the specialty of these sandwich shops, was the rarest and most exquisite tasting coffee in the world. I halted, as if I had suddenly bumped my head in my kitchen, much to the chagrin of others pushing through the door. They propelled me into this emporium, which I wanted to bypass and escape; the loudspeakers in my head kept the tune going, louder and louder. And strangely enough the tune took me, in memory, back to the hospital. I smelled the antiseptic; I could feel the texture of the bedsheets and see the nurses. It was just like Proust's account of the piece of cake he dipped into his tea one day and suddenly through taste recovered the profoundest memories of his childhood. The coffee tune had lain in wait within me for this moment of final treachery, for this door that belonged to the establishment that packaged, sold—and advertised—its coffee. It assured me, this tune, that I had come to the right place. What is more, I capitulated to my immediate need. Instead of walking out, I got my container of coffee. Then I fled.

Back in the chilly street, with my container of hot coffee in my hand, I had a moment of illumination. My thoughts ran like this: "Leon, you have been coffee-washed by the commercial, which you barely heard once or twice." And then: "If that supreme piece of damned nonsense is lodged so inextricably in your mind and memory, what is happening to the three-year-olds all over the nation sitting in front of their mechanical baby sitters? They are being coffee-washed before the age when they drink coffee. They are being soapsudded, they are being (or were) cigarette-induced." The principles of learning theory, the discoveries of Skinner, are being put to use on a stupendous scale: everything stated, repeated, reinforced, and all in a hodgepodge of discontinuity. A kind of terror seized me. I drank my coffee at my desk with a feeling that my inner world had been violated. Only when half an hour or an hour had elapsed did that tune cease to make itself heard.

I will not go into the full detail of the experiment I carried out during the next few days. How I tried to avoid that door, but heard the tune every time I passed it, how I entered telling myself I wouldn't hear it, and still it played louder than ever, and how I began to wonder whether it would ever be extinguished. Other revolving doors did not have this effect: so that the place itself, the brand name, was the trigger. All this renewed an old interest of mine in the psychology of learning. We know that in the same way in which we learn to walk at a certain age, we suddenly at a later moment open our ears to the world and it is at that moment that children can learn foreign languages, several at once, and without the accent adults have to struggle with at a still later stage. A well-known American writer told me that he had been born in China and passed some part of his boyhood there. He had known a little Chinese as a child, but had forgotten it. Nevertheless, when he revisited the little town, the Chinese words arose out of his past to serve his needs, triggered by the revisited environment.

And so I satisfied myself that the media, in which the young in particular are immersed, are much more than the transient casual amusing thing we consider them in our society. The media are more than entertainment. They educate. They rub things into us. I may say that it took me days and days of careful avoidance of that coffee shop before I finally toned down that tune. As a commercial it was a failure; it didn't sell me any more of that coffee. But as a transmitted message, it was a gross success. Even today I believe the erasure to be only partial.

III

Well, let me come out of the revolving door. I want to appraise this little adventure, so personal yet so vivid, which I lived that summer in the aftermath of my days with a television set in a hospital room. It can be said that in an older time—and even today although the experience is more rare—our vision, our ears, our nerves, our sense of smell, our touch, were exposed to human things around us, not in an artificial and kaleidoscopic way, but simply by their presence—a bird on a lawn, a cloud in the sky, a cluster of trees. We assimilated a human landscape, or a landscape which became humanized for us through our familiarity with it. If we read a book we performed an act that involved our attention, seeing words, grasping meanings, relating them to one another; we did not sit and "vision" the book. The pages were not turned for us. The book might have been trivial, but the assimilation of it belonged to a process of human action and human energy. Knowing what the older landscapes of the interior were, try to imagine the interior landscape of those exposed to a continuum of supersuds and colas. Certain of our young have had planted ineradicably within them a world of discontinuous jittery things, of girls dancing on the sand because they are about to drink a bubbling drink that pours itself automatically into a glass; of a man seriously talking about the wonders of cigarettes or

gasoline and minutes later the President of the United
States talking in the same manner about politics as
if politics too were cigarettes or gasoline. Children
watching at a tender age cannot differentiate; it is all
a clutter, and the received landscape is an erratic
phantasmagoric evanescent—yet recalled—landscape.
Long ago Flaubert tried to compile a dictionary of
what he called "received ideas." One can imagine
what a bizarre task he would have today with received
images as well. Small wonder that some part of our
young—that part brutalized or vacuumized by the
audiovisual—wants larger-than-life posters of tomato
soup. It is called Pop Art but what it is, in reality,
is an attempt to recover the lost childhood of the TV
set, in which the tomato soup can looked so large
within the shimmering little box. Small wonder that
certain of our young want education to be given them
as things are given on a screen, without the effort of
reading and learning: want to chatter inconsequently,
as the box chatters and has chattered endlessly, in
every house or apartment, sometimes in several rooms
at once.

The landscapes of childhood incorporated into ourselves become the landscapes of our lives. And if I,
an adult of the pre-television age, could be so suscepti-
ble to that bit of commercial to which I unthinkingly
and innocently exposed myself, I can only conclude
that we are witnessing massive pollution of the inner
worlds of our generation. We may solve the problems
of our waning oxygen: science may learn how to demer-
curize fish; but unless we actively turn off, or moderate
the media, there is little hope for the ecology of
humanism; no amount of theorizing about the

inadequacies of our educational system, no amount
of Ford Foundation studies, no amount of congres-
sional hearings on the effects of violence on television—effects too obvious really all around us—can
alter the erosion of the human consciousness which
the mass media now is achieving and has achieved.
The question is formidable for those of us who have
escaped some part of the universal brainwash. These
persons alone know what is being lost; these alone
can grasp the failures in cognition-systems. These must
act, or surrender all that we have valued in our civilization, surrender to the deodorants and quiz education.

And so, by walking through a revolving door, I had
this painful illumination, and out of this isolated
experience, extremely personal, I have been able to
glimpse a whole generation caught in revolving doors,
a generation less fortunate than I was, because I could
find a way out, whereas the mass-produced minds of
the mass media are doomed to remain in the revolving
door, in a Dali-like landscape, of which the clocks
are bent, the rocks are bare, the desert stretches to
the sky, and the sky is monotone yet periodically
broken by the monotonously flashing iridescence of
strobe lights, which make everyone feel that there is
some kind of movement, some stirring in the dead
land. We are the spectators of a tragedy not yet fully
understood. We saw it in the erratic outbursts of youthful activists which developed, for a season, a kind of
instant activism and then turned off as if it were all
functioning through the turning of a dial. The greening
of America had in it a great deal of hugging of the
microphone, as if for security; and the green was
painted on. At one moment a brave revolutionary pro-

173

claimed the era of change with all the microphones of all the stations carrying his ungrammatical sentences to the world. And then, the next day, the microphones went away, and the hero was left standing there as it were naked, amid green-painted potted plants. The prophet had had his moment of glory. He had emitted a few words magnified by microphones. The glory would have to suffice for a lifetime. The microphones were elsewhere, looking for more verdancy.

In a prophecy of the future, Matthew Arnold said, "Grant that the supposed knowledge disappears, its power of being made to engage the emotions will disappear along with it"; but, he added, "the emotions will remain."

And here we come to the profound problem which modern psychology has studied, but which the public has not grasped. The emotions will remain, and something will have to be done about them. They can be drugged; they can be tranquilized, but on the morrow they áre still with us. We can see this among certain of the unhappy young, those who have been the unknowing victims of the media, and who have learned to live by incantation, or by parroting messages that ring in their ears. For some an awareness, an intuition, of their noisy vacuum exists. They feel angry, hurt, frustrated, deprived, unloved, dependent, a whole harpsichord of their being has been played upon and without anything emerging except the need of slightly delayed instant reply. They reach for the anodyne— drug or soda pop; drugs magnify good feelings and give them a false sense of living, and deaden pain; but they can also magnify the bad feelings. Or some of the young accept the occult. That is magic, the

extra-human; it helps in a quest for the mysteries of
life, for in the media there are no mysteries. Science
seems to make everything right.

And so if the ecology of humanism has been polluted,
we have to listen to the voice of the airmen who, having
to carry lives with them in their voyages, remind themselves as they prepare their computers, "garbage in,
garbage out." The question we must ask is what have
our secular universities achieved in the garbage disposal. So far as I can see, they have allowed themselves
to be choked by it. They turn out in force for the news-
paperized personalities; they provide audiences for
them. They build bigger communication centers—that
is, centers of further erosion. Doubtless the time will
come when Cosmic Martha will receive an honorary
degree, and doubtless she will be asked to meet a
seminar and be questioned about her cosmic thoughts.
Every fad, every popularized magnified personality,
has been offered the campus microphones when not
the campus television. The media have turned our
campuses topsy-turvy—those campuses which were
to be the harbingers of culture, the appraisers of experience and of the learning which experience makes possible. But we tend to shrug off experience. We start
each day as if it were freshly made, and this means
that we busy ourselves creating what has been created.
We make the old and call it new; and it is instant-new.

"In cognition," said Marshall McLuhan, "we have
to interiorize the exterior world. We have to recreate
in the medium of our senses and inner faculties the
frame of existence ... In speech we make or *poet* the
world even as we may say that the movie parrots the
world. Languages themselves are thus the greatest

works of art. They are the collective hymns to existence. For in cognition itself is the whole of the poetic
process. But the artist differs from most men in his
power to arrest and then reverse the stages of human
appreciation. He learns how to embody the stages of
cognition in an exterior work that can be held up for
contemplation."

And Mr. McLuhan went on to say these terrible
words; at least I find them terrible:

"Modern technology presumes to attempt a total
transformation of man and his environment. This calls
for an inspection and defense of all human values."

How are we to overcome this pollution of mind and
spirit? A pollution undreamed of in all man's history.
The polluted mind no longer has the ability to think
freely; it is a programmed mind and against such a
mind one cannot even pit a machine. The little box
has ended up as an educator; the medium becomes
the ecology of the message. We see only where the
camera looks; we do not see the scene without its
setting, and the medium has set the scene. When young
people reach the University, the teacher finds himself
confronted with an individual so programmed that he
is beyond learning; he may learn a few facts, but the
fundamentals, whatever they may be, have been frozen
into their personalities. Some of our young keep saying
they want to change the system, but what they are
asking for, in their helpless intuitive way, is for an
alteration in their programming. Never in all the uses
of the word "determinism" has the environment of
the mind been so determined and reinforced. We must
address ourselves promptly and in the most drastic
ways to ridding ourselves of instant barbarism: it floods

our homes and our mental atmosphere, surrounds us seemingly beyond reclaim.

And yet I do not say this in an utterly hopeless voice. There is a saving remnant of the population that has not been contaminated: we have demonstrated that with sufficient social action certain commercials can be taken off the air—as was done with cigarettes. We know that the older and wiser civilizations from the beginning understood—along with the totalitarian countries—the nature of the media: and that is why the BBC, the CBC, and such instruments as the Radiodiffusion Francaise or our own Educational Television were created. Let us not fear being accused of censorship; we know we are not trying to censor, but to reform; let us remember that we fight for the greatest freedom of all—the freedom from delusion. The press, which can turn a woman into a cosmic comic, has also demonstrated in the past, in time of war, that it understands the meaning of responsibility. It is possible to reform the media and to insist that they serve the values that enhance rather than degrade life. The media are so powerful that they must not be left in the hands of minds dedicated to salesmanship at all costs—not least at the cost of truth. Films too must be reformed: for we must recognize that control of the picture is not the same as control of the printed word. The dehumanization of sex and love, the technologizing of the erotic, illustrates what I mean. The Polynesians in a culture of the stone age had a more civilized attitude toward the erotic than we have. I have yet to see an erotic film that can convey the warmth and good humor that we discover in certain erotic hulas. Let us restore to the human that which is human; and let us render unto the machine that which is the machine's—but let us not give to the machine that authority it has derived from the false worship of science in our age.

I cannot close without reminding you that in poetry you will find the distilled wisdom of the ages; and John Donne, without the presence of television, understood well the meaning of inner landscapes of which I have spoken tonight. In one of his great verse letters he writes:

> Man is a lumpe, where all beasts kneaded bee
> Wisdom makes him an Arke where all agree;
> The foole, in whom these beasts do live at jarre,
> Is sport to others and a Theater.

We have created a mechanical box filled with beasts that in their discontinuous being and irrelevance "live at jarre"; these become our personal beasts as we absorb and clutter our own being with them; and they make fools of us. Which makes us "sport to others and a Theater"—the press calls this news. And daily the cameras and microphones arrive to record this Theater of tomfoolery, so that the folly is constantly compounded. Watching the antics in the metal box, people perform antics. And Donne adds:

> How happy is hee, which hath due place assigned
> To his beasts, and disaforested his minde!

We must disaforest the mind of our time, or become jungle.

What I am saying is that the camera is to the ecology of humanism what the automobile has been to our physical ecology. The car, along with other pollutants, has set going a chain reaction the end of which we cannot yet foresee; camera-reality has undermined the delicate ecology of the human imagination, the arts, learning, the creative intelligence. Marianne Moore, you will remember, in a famous poem, spoke of poetry as "imaginary gardens with real toads in them." The media have put real toads in real gardens; but they have covered our eyes with camera lenses. Moreover, we have no control over the angle shots, the close-ups, and we haven't the freedom of vision to determine our own angles. It is time we uncovered our eyes and started looking again at real toads and imagined gardens. Only in this way will we be able to step out of the revolving doors.